KU-208-457

Group Training for Individual and Organizational Development

Group Training
for Individual and Organizational
Development

Editor: Cary L. Cooper, Southampton

1 figure, 10 tables

S. Karger · Basel · München · Paris · London · New York · Sydney · 1972

Reprint from 'Interpersonal Development', Vol. 3, No. 1–4 (1972)

S. Karger · Basel · München · Paris · London · New York · Sydney
Arnold-Böcklin-Strasse 25, CH–4011 Basel (Switzerland)

All rights, including that of translation into other languages, reserved. Photomechanic reproduction (photocopy, microcopy) of this book or parts thereof without special permission of the publishers is prohibited.

©   Copyright 1972 by S. Karger AG, Verlag für Medizin und Naturwissenschaften, Basel
Printed in Switzerland
ISBN 3–8055–1481–6

Contents

Acknowledgements

The Editor wishes to offer his sincere thanks to all the contributors to this book. In addition, he would also like to extend his appreciation to the indexer, *Diana Marshallsay,* and to his secretary and typist *Alison Steele.*

Interpers. Develop. *3:* 7–12 (1972)

Introduction: The Methods and Aims of Group Training

C.L. Cooper

The following is an excerpt[1] from a session of a T-group run for a top management team of a large, heavy-manufacturing plant in the north of England. The work roles of the various people described below are: Eric, Plant Director; John, Joint Deputy Plant Director; Bill, Joint Deputy Plant Director; Nicholas, Works Engineer; Harry, Commercial Manager; Consultant, T-group trainer and Management Consultant.

Nicholas: 'You (Bill) say that John and Eric are on the beam all the time, I'm not too sure, I wonder if John really does think like Eric, often John seems to agree with Eric a little too readily – so quickly that he cannot really have thought about it at all.'

Eric: 'No, that's quite unfair, I don't see the relationship with John in the same way you do, Nicholas. I feel that I sometimes follow John. Often when I reflect at the end of the day I realise that it's John who has got his way and not the other way around, not a case of him coming in too early, a case of him leading me along.'

Consultant: 'What is it that you are saying, Eric? Are you explaining that what Nicholas feels is not the way it is? If I were a full-time member of this group I'd be a little concerned about the relationship between you two.'

John: 'Yes, it's a good point that Nicholas brought up. He sees the role I play opposite Eric as being different from the role I play opposite other people. Sometimes in the short run I might appear to go along with Eric – that's while I think it through, in the long run, you know, I sometimes disagree.'

Nicholas: 'This may be so but on occasions I have felt that you have gone along with Eric even when you didn't agree. In short I feel that Eric can control this group; the two of you together are a formidable force.'

John: 'I do feel more sympathetic to Eric than to others; Harry would come at the bottom of any hierarchy of sympathy, in between, is Bill and you Nicholas. I have sympathy with Eric because he works bloody hard. I have a sense of values and this is damned important to me – working hard, but secondly, he's an effective thinker, therefore I listen to him, I try to understand, whereas with Harry, after listening for a long time I certainly can't understand him.'

1 A brief extract of an article by *Mangham, I.L.; Hayes, J., and Cooper, C.L.:* Developing executive relationships: six characters in search of a management style. Interpers. Develop. *1:* 110–127 (1970).

Nicholas: 'However, with me, occasionally you have been jocular and sort of down-putting, and this bloody irritates me.'

John: 'Well, why don't you say so at the time?'

Nicholas: 'Because I feel blocked out, by you two sitting up there smiling at each other, in the know, in each other's pockets all the time. It's bloody difficult for anyone else to get a point of view across. It does surprise me sometimes, that you had been putting pressure on Harry. I remember two or three weeks ago I got bloody angry toward you, John, about some issue but basically it was because I saw you as putting a hell of a lot of pressure on Harry.'

John: 'Well, you seeing that sort of thing upsets me because I honestly didn't know we were putting that much pressure on Harry, really I didn't, Eric might have noticed it but I did not.'

Eric (returning to the issue of the special relationships): 'I can't quite see how this special relationship that John and I are supposed to have can cause problems for the rest of the group. It might be useful to have a look at other people's relationship with me in the group, as I see them anyway. Maybe they'd like to say something about it after I've finished. Bill – you see, I'm really very neutral towards you, Bill – this could be one of the problems that's facing this group. As I see it, you don't appear to have built any relationships within the group – you have some sort of relationships outside. There's no meaningful ones within the group. Harry, well, we've said a lot about that relationship. You, Nicholas, well, there have been a few problems, not many. You're learning you know. You've made a few mistakes for example, with the shop stewards. You made me mad on occasions but you're doing alright, you're coming along.'

Consultant: 'Nicholas, how do you feel about that?'

Nicholas: 'Like a schoolboy being patted on the head by the headmaster. It's as if Eric is saying to me "you're an up and coming young lad, not yet in the same league as John but you're doing alright".'

Eric: 'Well, that's the way it is, I'm sorry – you know, in my opinion Nicholas, you have done well, in my opinion you aren't yet dealing with the same issues, thinking in the same way as John and I. If it's a question of you being in this group then I'm one hundred per cent for it.'

John: 'And this is really what we're still discussing, whether or not we want this group to exist at all, and if so, who's to be in.'

Consultant: 'Well, it seems to me that the two people you are very uncertain about, and who are uncertain about their own position in all of this are Bill and Harry. Before you try to gain their full commitment to the group or to imply their rejection, it might be useful if you could spell out the pros and cons of their commitment. What's in it for them?'

Eric: 'I said before and I'm going to repeat it now, that really the only way forward is to make a frank assessment and I expect the same and am willing to accept the same being done on me. As I see it, Bill and Harry have little to gain in terms of promotion so this group isn't going to be a stepping stone to anything else. The only reward can be intrinsic, neither Bill nor Harry have a future outside this plant as far as I know, unless they leave the company altogether. For John – I would say he is the company's next Plant Director, and there's no doubt about that. He's very intelligent, a very capable man and he's just about the right sort of age. He's got all the energy, all the drive, everything that's necessary to make a plant director. He'd make a hell of a lot better manager here than I do. Nicholas, well again, very unsure: young enough, has got enough ability, but the whole role of the engineer, and whole company structure is, as you know, currently in turmoil. Could be that this group will be very useful for him, to help him move into the area of general management, so it can make the transition to assistant plant director, or even to plant director at some stage much easier for him. So for two of the people, Bill and Harry, the group holds no attractions in terms of extrinsic rewards, it holds the attraction of being in something that makes the decisions, that implements them, that looks ahead, and that works in the very ambiguous area of general management. But the reward must essentially be inside themselves. Is this the sort of thing they really want to be doing with their time? For the other two it can clearly be of intrinsic and extrinsic use – it can give them satisfaction, it can also provide a platform for moving on. Now I can understand how many pressures there are, especially as you get older; when you're young your wife doesn't mind so much the long hours. They're expected if you're going to get on, but remember they become less sympathetic when you've reached your career ceiling. When that happens it is time to make the decision. I see this group as being one that has to meet frequently, one that has to make big decisions, one that has to take time, one which has to check out, one which has really got to learn to work together. Make no mistake about it, I basically want to work together, you see, people are one of my problems. I have accused John earlier of being unemotional but I feel that really unemotional one is me. I have to work with lots of people and I keep getting in the same sort of problems we've been talking about – these last two or three days. I just keep getting in these problems and I want to get out of them, and this group can help me do that. They can help me understand me, and they can help me become a better plant director.'

Consultant: 'Well, you've said something about what might be in it for other people, Eric, what's in it for you?'

Nicholas: 'That's the question I was just about to ask.'

Eric: 'Well, what's in it for me. I'm not viewing the success of this group as some sort of vehicle for promotion, no, I'm well past that sort of position, I'm not even sure that if it were offered to me I would want to take it. In some ways this group idea runs counter to what the company thinks about the way to work. In general, the boys upstairs think we should just tell people what to do. We shouldn't discuss things with them, we shouldn't try to talk things through, so I don't think they would look very favourably on it. Even if I were in the position to be promoted, anyway – and I am at the point of not really wanting to go further, not wanting to do anything else, other than just be a good plant director here – team work would not be viewed favourably. What will it do to me in other ways? I think it will make life a hell of a lot easier, because being at the top in an organization like this is – it's a cliché, I know – a bloody lonely job, and I just want to be able to talk to people to get things sorted out, to be able to get good and honest advice. That's what I want out of it, to be part of something, not trapped in a cold image of the boss, somebody who tells you to do things. You see, I think that at the top it should be a sort of "we" thing, not an "I". We should want to do something, we should agree to it, not I want you to do something for me.'

This short extract, taken from a session of an in-company T-group, illustrates some of the features of the educational technique referred to as Sensitivity or T-group Training. Firstly, as *Tannenbaum et al.* (4) have indicated, the training is primarily 'process-orientated' as distinct from 'content-orientated'. That is, the primary stress is on the feeling level of communications between people rather than on the informational or conceptual. Individuals are encouraged to deal with their feelings about themselves and others and to explore the impact they have upon each other. They examine feelings, expressions, gestures, and subtle behaviours which in everyday life often are taken for granted. Second, the training is not structured in a conventional manner. The staff member does not provide the group with a topic of conversation. The individual members must decide themselves what they want to talk about, what kinds of problems they wish to deal with, and what means they want to use in reaching their goals. As they concern themselves with these problems, they begin to act in characteristic ways: some people remain silent, some are aggressive, some tend consistently to initiate discussion, and some attempt to structure the proceedings. With the aid of the staff member, these approaches or developments become the focal points for discussion and analysis. The staff member draws attention to events and behaviour in the group by occasional interventions in the form of tentative interpretations which he considers will provide information for study. He encourages members to focus attention on behaviour in the group, here and now. Who is behaving in what way and what feelings are being generated as a result? Third, the heart of a T-group laboratory is found in small groups, allowing a high level of participation, involvement and free communication. These groups therefore consist of between eight to 12 members.

As *Smith* (3) has suggested, any T-group, as any natural group, has a number of problems toward which its attention is focused. Some of these are:

The problem of distribution of power and influence: Shall the group be tightly structured? Shall it be informal and unplanned? Who shall determine this? How shall the group deal with the staff member's power and influence?

The problem of intimacy: How much of my private thoughts and feelings is it right to tell the group? How close shall the group members become to one another?

The problem of identity: What sort of person am I? How do I compare with these other group members? What is the 'real' me — me as I see me, or as they can see me?

As the group works on these problems, it develops a normative structure or set of rules governing the range of permissible behaviours, a more open and trusting environment, and a less defensive one. When this occurs it is possible for group members to give and receive feedback with regard to one another's behaviour. The feedback process is one whereby a member of the group is told by the others what effect his behaviour has had on them. As *Smith* (3) has illustrated, individuals in the group learn that the sort of feedback that is usable by the receiver does not comprise general value judgments ('I think that you are an aggressive s.o.b.') but specific statements as to what feelings and behaviour followed an act of the receiver's ('When you proposed that you should be chairman, I was very angry, but I said nothing because I feared the consequences'). In this way, each member of the group builds up a picture of how the others respond to his customary behaviour. Meaningful and accurate communication necessitates this kind of checking of messages which is rarely possible in ordinary everyday life.

As you might be able to predict, there are a number of possible outcomes of this form of training. *Miles* (1) summarised a number of these as increases in:

'*Sensitivity:* the ability to perceive what is actually going on in a social situation (including both behavioural events and inferred feelings of other persons).

'*Diagnostic ability:* the skill of assessing ongoing social situations in a way that enables effective action; the employment of appropriate explanatory categories to understand reasons for presented interaction.

'*Action skill:* the ability to intervene effectively in ongoing situations in such a way as to maximise personal and group effectiveness and satisfaction ...'

All these T-group training goals have one thing in common: they are directed toward developing the individual; helping him to become more aware of himself and his impact on others, to behave more effectively in face-to-face situations, and to re-assess his fundamental interpersonal approach (specifically in relation to his needs of power, affection, and aggression). In addition to these objectives, there are at least two others. Firstly, as *Redlich and Astrachan* (2) emphasise, in an issue of the American Journal of Psychiatry dealing specifically with this form of training, T-groups can increase one's understanding of the psychology of group and intergroup behaviour. In this context, the concepts of role differentiation, group normative structure, and authority relationships can be explored in the course of the development of this ongoing self-analytic group. Thus, the skills of people in observing group and intergroup behaviour can be enhanced.

And secondly, another primary aim of T-group training is 'to improve team-work within the organization' — to develop the organization as a team rather than the individual as a person, as in the illustration at the beginning of this article. In this situation, one would assemble for discussion of interpersonal problems on the job, an ongoing work group; the group might include, for instance, an industrial manager and his subordinates; or a senior social worker and his/her social workers under supervision; or any other group of people who work together and whose interpersonal relationships may be or are preventing them from performing their work effectively. This area of interest is commonly referred to as 'organizational development'.

Broadly speaking, therefore, the T-group approach can and has been used to achieve a number of different outcomes which can crudely be divided into three categories: learning about one's self, learning about group and intergroup dynamics, and improving work group relations. These objectives are not achieved by relying on a standard T-group training design, although a number of constituents of the method described earlier are common to all such designs. This form of training requires careful specification of the goal or problem in a particular situation and the creation of a training design which will meet these goals or resolve problems. In addition, the training programme required to achieve a particular goal can vary greatly from situation to situation. For example, a training programme to improve work group relations among a group of waiters and waitresses might differ substantially in design from one for the board of directors of a large multi-national industrial organization. The objectives of the training may be relatively similar — to reduce interpersonal obstacles and improve the work-group or organizational climate — but the approach employed may, within limits, differ in quite a number of ways: in the balance of conceptual and experiential learning; in the inclusion or exclusion of boss, subordinates, colleagues, or related staff; in the orientation of the training staff (person-centred vs. group-centred), etc.

This leads us to the purposes of this volume. It is the intention here to provide people who have used the T-group and related group training methods in particular situations, an opportunity of describing why they have used them and how they designed their training programmes to achieve their particular objectives. The various articles will illustrate the efforts of the trainers to meet one or some combination of the T-group aims outlined in previous paragraphs. In addition, one will be able to see how different training designs and approaches have been used in totally different social contexts attempting to achieve roughly similar objectives. For example, the articles on group training in industry and in a psychiatric hospital both illustrate attempts at achieving one of the primary aims of the T-group method, the improvement of interpersonal work relationships. The training styles, however, are, as you will see, quite different. This may be due to differences in objectives of the organization, in their social milieu, and in role relationships inherent in the organization. And finally, an attempt will be made to provide the widest possible coverage of this training in a variety of different situations, i.e. industry (manufacturing and service), hospitals, the social services, the civil service, among youth, and in society at large.

Let me conclude by saying that most of the case studies and descriptive material presented here reflect current applications of this form of training and, in some cases, a bold effort of introducing programmes of individual and organizational change into environments which have previously been static and less than innovative.

References

1   *Miles, M.:* Human relations training. Processes and outcomes. J. Counsel. Psychol. *7:* 301–306 (1960).
2   *Redlich, F.C. and Astrachan, B.:* Group dynamics training. Amer. J. Psychiat. *125:* 1501–1507 (1969).
3   *Smith, P.B.:* The use of T-groups in effecting individual and organizational change. Psychol. Scene *1:* 23–26 (1967).
4   *Tannenbaum, R.; Weschler, I.R., and Massarik, F.:* Leadership and organization (McGraw-Hill, New York 1961).

Author's address: Dr. *Cary L. Cooper,* Department of Psychology, The University, *Southampton SO9 5NH* (England)

Interpers. Develop. *3:* 13–39 (1972)

Group Training in a Service Industry: Improving Social Skills in Motorway Service Area Restaurants[1]

C.L. Cooper and H. Oddie

Department of Psychology, University of Southampton, Southampton

Introduction

By statute, all firms in the United Kingdom employing over a minimum number of personnel in every industry are required to contribute a percentage of their annual wage bill towards the organisation, development and administration of training within their particular industry. The actual amount levied is determined by levying bodies called Industry Training Boards who are empowered to control and direct all training within their respective industries. The Hotel and Catering Industry Training Board (HCITB) is one such body and is responsible for training and research for all hotels, restaurants, cafeterias, snack bars and allied activities in the whole of the British Isles.

In late 1969, the HCITB contacted the authors asking them if they would examine the feasibility of providing group training in social skills for food service operatives (i.e. waiters, waitresses, chefs, etc.). The HCITB recognised that customers in restaurants and cafeterias are sensitive to the way in which staff relate to them in the course of their duties. Most trainers within the Board agreed that group training in interpersonal relations or social skills was desirable. The request therefore was for guidance on the form and method of training. In addition, the HCITB felt that research should be carried out to evaluate the effect of this training so that the development of social skill training within the industry might evolve in an orderly and efficient manner. The present article describes the authors' effort at achieving these aims. Specifically, the aims were: (1) to design courses which represent different approaches to group training in social skills but whose objectives are in line with the needs of the industry; (2) to evaluate by means of a controlled study the relative usefulness of these approaches. It was hoped that the result of these efforts would be to provide a reservoir of experi-

1 The authors would like to thank the Hotel and Catering Industry Training Board and the Department of Employment (UK) for their support in this project.

ence in the day-to-day operation of social skill training courses for the HCITB that could be drawn on by the catering industry at large. In addition, it was hoped that it would be possible to monitor the reaction of the industry (as represented by the host company) to group training in social skills and its effects.

The purpose of this article is to describe the group training programmes devised for the catering industry and the research design (including the measures and results) utilised to evaluate them.

Relevant Research prior to the Present Project

Studies within the Hotel and Catering Industry

Whyte (17) pioneered the application of the 'human relations' approach to the hotel and catering industry. He highlighted the 'crisis of authority' characteristic of the industry and was the first to analyse customer/staff relations and describe potential 'flashpoints' within a typical restaurant work team. However, *Whyte* did not propose training programmes to help resolve the problems he had delineated, he was interested only in drawing attention to the dynamics of the restaurant as a social organisation.

Pickard et al. (12) interested themselves in the application of social relations theory to training techniques in the catering industry. However, their study did not go much further than offering tentative suggestions about the general direction trainers should be moving in. A much more determined approach was made by *Damodaran* (6) who mounted a small action training and research programme consisting of group discussions, lectures, seminars and practical exercises. The objectives of this training were stated 'to train people (i.e. waiters, waitresses, etc.) to be more adaptable and more skilled in the customer contact area. Also to improve job satisfaction and staff awareness of organisational problems'. Although the project had certain limitations — it was based on a single restaurant and the research worker conducting the evaluation was also administering the training programme — it did give promise of some interesting results. Unfortunately, the research programme had to be seriously curtailed and the final evaluation stage omitted.

It was clear that very little research into group training for social skills had taken place within the catering industry and, in particular, there was a conspicuous absence of clearly designed social skill courses.

Studies in Related Fields

Outside the hotel and catering industry, there have been a number of studies concerned with organisation development and managerial improvement. Typical of such studies is that of *Buchanan and Brunstetter* (2). It is clear from the outline of their programme goals that they were very much interested in developing *social skills* within an organisational context. The second of two major goals is described thus: 'Facilitate development of peoples ... (a) perceptiveness of social situations and process, (b) skill and creativeness in problem solving, (c) flexibility of behaviour.' This study is important because it applies the philosophy and method of scientific research to social skill training. The researchers proceeded by first presenting their training goals and isolating the assumptions behind the change process in the organisational setting. They next related their goals to the context of the organisation for which the development programme was being instituted. The programme itself was conceived in research terms in that the design allowed for a controlled evaluation of the training outcomes against the stated goals.

While *Buchanan and Brunstetter* and similar studies throughout the 1960s focussed on organisational development, a parallel series concerned itself with the individual trainee (3, 10). However, training method and philosophy in all these studies were very similar. All were primarily interested in the development of training techniques and methods of evaluation in human relations, whether the research focussed on the individual or on the organisation. Thus, in one study, *Valiquet* (15) looked specifically at individual changes in what was essentially a management (organisational) development programme.

The project reported here derives its basic rationale and evaluative techniques from these two traditions. It builds on the work already done by extending the application of training for interpersonal relations beyond the managerial and supervisory levels to that of the operative and by essaying refinements of the evaluation tools developed by *Bunker* (3), *Harrison* (8) and *Van der Vegt* (16).

Two Approaches to Group Training in Social Skills

Any survey of the literature of group training in social skill techniques reveals an interesting dichotomy. The different approaches can nearly always be assigned to one of two categories which are each based on a different underlying training philosophy. Essentially, one approach sees this training as primarily *skill* training, that is, social skills are acquired in much the same way as motor skills — one learns to get on better with customers and colleagues by similar methods as one learns to drive an automobile. This approach is based on *Argyle*'s (1) conception and model of interpersonal behaviour in terms of motor skills. The other approach (fostered by National Training Laboratory) stresses the *social* rather than the *skill* aspect of interpersonal interactions. Training, according to this approach, has to be 'process-orientated' rather than 'content-orientated' (14), and people are seen to improve their social skills by studying their own behaviour through observing interaction and receiving direct feedback within an ongoing small group situation. The main distinction between the two approaches is that the latter is person-centred, whereas the former asserts that social skill acquisition can occur without focussing on the trainee as a person. It is this dichotomy of training philosophies that forms the basis of the training programmes utilised in this project.

The Research Design

The main features of our research design were as follows:

(1) There would be two programmes of group training in social skills based on the two different training methods.

(2) *Programme A* (*skills* course) would be developed out of an earlier HCITB course and would essentially be teaching techniques and social skills that would be useful to participants when they returned to their work situations. The teaching methods employed would be 'traditional', that is, they would use primarily group discussion of social skills and work problems supported by ancillary group techniques of role-playing, 'learning by example', exercises and projects to be completed by groups of participants. The development and running of this programme would be in the hands of the consultants who developed the earlier HCITB courses.

(3) *Programme B* (*social* course) would have a different starting point. It would be centred around the T-group approach to social skill training. The emphasis would be on learning by participating in and observing ongoing group interaction. The courses would be run by consultants experienced in and committed to this training technique.

(4) Each programme would consist of seven one-week courses. All would take place over the same time period (two months) and at two independent training centres.

(5) Evaluation would consist of four measurement samples. The first sample to be taken a few weeks prior to training; the second on the first day of each course; the third on the last day of each course; and the fourth and final sample would be taken three to five months after the training programme had ended.

Before going on to discuss the programmes in more detail, there are two areas that need to be described. The first area is that of goals and assumptions of the training; the second is the specific context in which training was to take place.

Training Goals

Many theorists have outlined a number of training goals in group training for social skills (2, 4, 13). There will be no attempt to look at these in detail here, but the reader will find a useful summary in *Cooper and Mangham* (5).

In the present study, it was felt that a slavish adherence to any of the above lists of training goals would not be helpful, since (1) this was an industrial project and the training had to be related to the specific needs of the parent industry; (2) because the project was a field study sited with a specific company, the needs of this organisation had to be taken into account; (3) and finally, as the two programmes were to be run by two independent teams of consultants, it was felt that each team should have a certain amount of freedom in formulating their own training programmes. This allowed differences between the methodologies to be accentuated and it also maintained a high level of personal commitment to the respective programmes by the consultants — which helped to facilitate relations between the training and the research side of the project. In the main, it amounted to letting the trainers 'do their own thing' within the bounds dictated by the industry's and the company's training needs.

The company's needs were not formally stated but were generated by a number of liaison meetings involving research staff, HCITB officials, consultants, company training personnel and company site management. The industry's needs were canvassed by the researchers prior to the project's commencement and with the aid of HCITB officers. Although only a small sample was used, a broad cross-section of the industry and its related training bodies were aimed at. The kinds of social skill training outcomes deemed desirable by the industry on the basis of our short survey included: (1) increased perceptiveness of social cues; (2) increased understanding of inter- and intra-working group relations; (3) improved performances of behavioural skills related to social cues; (4) increased awareness and understanding of social norms operating in the work environment; (5) a general increase in the sensitivity of staff to their social environment. These proved useful guidelines to the training consultants and researchers.

The Industrial Context

For research purposes, we required a host company who could provide a number of similar sites which could form our research population and from which a research sample could be extracted. Ideally, we wanted (1) sites which provided a variety of catering activities, (2) which had a range of workroles to create a wide base for generalisations of the research findings, (3) sites which would be typical of a broad section of the industry, and, (4) at the same time, we needed an organisation with sub-populations that were relatively balanced with regard to function, structure, management/staff ratio, etc.

The Sites

Four sites were chosen. All belonged to the motorway division of an international hotel and catering organisation. The four establishments were all situ-

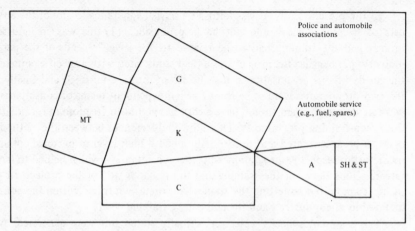

Fig. 1. MT = motor transport cafeteria; G = grill and restaurant; C = cafeteria; K = kitchen; A = administration offices; SH & ST = shop and stores.

ated along the UK main North–South highway, the M-1 motorway. Since the M-1 carries such a large volume of traffic, activities contained within the motorway service areas (restaurants, petrol service, etc.) have to comply to very strict government regulations. There are, therefore, both strong statutory and environmental pressures on motorway service areas to maintain organisational conformity.

A typical service area consists of several interlocking service units. The sites we chose had the basic layout shown in figure 1.

As can be seen, the basic motorway site unit consists of a kitchen, motor transport cafeteria, public cafeteria, grill and restaurant, and a 'peripheral' service area (i.e. the fuel and spares' services, shop, stores, motoring organisation offices, motorway personnel depots and police stations). Some of these peripheral site activities are not under the control of the operating company but, nevertheless, there has to be liaison with them and they make from time to time demands on the organisation. For training and research purposes, the authors were mainly concerned with the grill and restaurant and cafeteria areas.

Staffing

Because the sites are generally away from urban areas, staff often have to travel some distance to get to work. The company in fact usually made special transport arrangements because of this. There are three shifts – two day shifts and a night shift – and staff tend to be permanently assigned to one shift. For training and research purposes, only the day shifts were used. There were on average 10–12 personnel per unit per shift and a typical breakdown is given as follows.

Grill and restaurant	1 manager/manageress
	1 griddler
	1 cold-bar assistant
	1 or 2 receptionist/cashier
	7 waitresses (approx. 20 tables per station)
Public cafeteria (self-service)	1 manageress
	2 or 3 table receptionists
	1 griddler/cook
	1 beverage hand
	2 preparation hands
	1 cashier
Kitchen	1 manager
	1 cook (assistant manager)
	1 assistant cook
	2 preparation hands
	1–3 porters, including wash up

The Training Programmes

The Research Sample

Courses were run at independent training centres so that the centres were completely outside company influence. Because most participants had heavy home commitments, the courses were all non-residential. Special transport facilities were made available to all participants between their homes and the training centres. Participants were drawn from the staffs of the major units of grills and cafeterias. 106 persons participated in the training programme. Course membership was kept as heterogeneous (as the circumstances would allow) in terms of organisational roles. A typical course might consist of between 7–9 persons: a cashier, a table receptionist, a manageress, a counter assistant and three waitresses. Each programme consisted of 7 consecutively-run one-week courses.

The staff from the grills and cafeterias of two motorway sites underwent training along programme A lines and the trainees from two comparable sites were trained along programme B lines.

The Course Programmes and Schedules
Schedule A: The 'skill' course

Day 1	Introductions	Participants introduce themselves to each other.
	Motorway service	Discussion of what is involved in motorway service: 'the people' business.
	Social skill	Discussion: What is it? How socially skilled do participants consider themselves? How are social skills related to job performance?
	Assignment	Short exercise for participants on motorway service.

Day 2	Observing people	There's more to it than meets the eye!... Seeing is not believing: Lecture and group discussion on how we perceive other people.
	Understanding people	Closer observation; the kinds of social cues to look for in other people.
	Assignment	'As I see it' – exercise on perceiving others.
Day 3	First impressions	The art of making friends ... and getting on with the boss: Lecture and group discussion on forming impressions of people.
	Customer needs	Recognising and meeting needs.
	Assignment	Personal project work on getting on with customers and colleagues.
Day 4	Putting it over	How to give information.
	Dealing with customers	The Awkward, the Amorous, or the Merely Complaining.
	Assignment	Project work.
Day 5	Practical sessions	Customer/waiter role-playing exercise – feedback from other trainees.
	Personal appearances	Dress, make-up ... discussion of standards.
	Private sessions	What I do well ... and not so well!
	Summing up	Discussion: What to do next.
	Assignment	Project work.

The programme was a free one and varied to suit individual course needs. Assignments were often begun in class and completed in the evening. Each participant was provided with a folder in which course notes could be stored together with 'hand-outs' from the instructor. Each participant was given a course schedule.

Schedule B: The 'social' course: T-group orientation

Day 1	Introductions. Sharing and comparing perceptions of the participants' roles. Exploring differences, looking at stereotypes and noticing how various role functions relate to each other.
Day 2	Looking at interpersonal problems within a restaurant context. Exploring the similarities and differences of the problems faced by the members of different units.
Day 3	Direct focussing on the interpersonal behaviour of group members. Exercises to facilitate giving and receiving personal feedback.
Day 4	As for day 3.
Day 5	As for day 3, but with an emphasis on the development of 'action plans' related to the back-home situation.

A brief description of the main teaching technique was given by the consultants concerned: ' "Laboratory methods" are simply teaching techniques which utilise the data generated from the group of trainees. Thus the participants learn from their own experience as it is occurring ... participants learn *by doing* rather than by a passive, purely cognitive learning process.'

As stressed earlier, the consultants played a major part in moulding training goals. The consultants for programme B explicitly stated their formulation of training goals:

(1) To improve participants ability to work effectively with other members of his/her unit by: (a) facilitating more open communication between different roles and levels; (b) developing understanding of the functioning of work groups; (c) exploring differences in preception of the job situation and confronting role relationship problems.

(2) To increase participants' awareness of the impact of their own behaviour on others.

(3) To increase self- and other-awareness by examining and testing their assumptions and perceptions about their own role and behaviour — and of other people to whom they relate.

Evaluation Measures

A number of measures for assessing social skills have been described by researchers (5, 8). The basic approach of these researchers has been to sample the trainee's perception of himself and his associates' perception of his on-the-job behaviour. A similar approach was followed in the present study, although certain refinements had been made to the measurement instruments. Measurements were taken at four points in time (as discussed earlier) in the following areas:

(1) the trainee's perception of himself, his work associates, his trainer, and the course;

(2) work associates' perception of the trainee's behaviour on the job;

(3) the customer's perception of trainee service;

(4) labour turnover among trainees.

Perception Questionnaires

(a) Changes in perceived image (CPI). Bipolar adjectival scales similar to the *Osgood et al.* (11) measure were used, with the exception that the concepts were generated by the individual trainees, using a modified form of *Kelly*'s (9) role repertory test. The CPI comprised 7 forms, each containing the same 17-item bipolar scales. One of these forms was for self-rating, one for ideal-rating, four for rating other trainees, and one for rating the trainer. Each trainee rated the same individuals throughout the evaluation programme.

(b) Post-course critique (PCC), inventory of planned change (IPC), and inventory of planned change follow-up (IPCpQ). These 3 questionnaires are related to each other and will be considered together. The aim of the PCC was to record the subjective course assessments of the participants themselves. This post-course critique would examine 6 areas: (1) affective response of participants (whether they liked their course or not); (2) effective response of participants (whether the course helped them or not); (3) priority of course goals in participants' eyes (the importance of social skills to an individual's job); (4) perception of trainer by participants; (5) perception of trainer's technique (what they thought of the way the course was run by their instructor); (6) attitudes to course duration (too long versus too short). Each of these areas was examined by means of the 7-point bipolar scale. In order to get the participants to analyse in more detail their effective response, a check-list was included. There was also space for free response on this point.

Incorporated in the middle of the PCC was the IPC. Essentially, this asked the participant to make a list of any changes in personal behaviour he planned to make on returning to the work situation. This might be thought of as an inverted mini-*Bunker* (3) questionnaire, because the *Bunker* format (see the PCI below) was followed. Participants made a forced choice response (yes/no), followed by a free response, if they answered yes in the first part. Whereas *Bunker* asks about changes in the past, the IPC asks about *future* changes. In addition, the IPC asked participants to forecast the attitudes of their work associates to their changed behaviour.

The IPCpQ is the follow-up questionnaire to the IPC part of the PCC. Its aims are threefold: (1) to test retention of change plans; (2) to examine effectiveness of changes; (3) to discover how associates reacted to participants' changes. There was also a final free-response section allowing participants to reassess their course learning and to indicate the chief obstacles in the assimilation of learning into their behaviour at work.

The PCC and IPC were administered only to participants and this was done at noon on the final day of the course. The IPCpQ was included in the final evaluation session at follow-up.

Behaviour Change Questionnaires

(a) Perceived change inventory (PCI). This instrument measures behavioural aspects of training effects. It has been extensively used in other studies in this field over the past decade. Essentially, it is a list of specific changes, as perceived by an observer (in this case the trainee's work associates), of a given individual. The form that is generally used is the behavioural change inventory of *Bunker* (3). This is an open-ended questionnaire based on the design of *Miles* (10). It asks the observer (1) to say if behavioural change had occurred and (2) to describe in detail these changes. For the present project, certain modifications were made to the basic *Bunker-Miles* format. In the first place, observers or work associates were directed to look at two kinds of change: (1) change associated with how the trained person relates to his work associates and (2) change associated with how he relates to customers. In the second place, a rating of change is added for each set of descriptions. Thirdly, observers were encouraged to list any change they considered to be outside the scope of the above directions. The questionnaire also includes space for detailed examples of the changes mentioned. Up to five people reported on each member of the research sample and the average number of observers per person was 3.28. Each observed person also completed a self report in the PCI format.

(b) Perceived functional image questionnaire (PFI). The original instrument was in essence an organisational questionnaire. It sought to establish how the respondent viewed the organisation in which he worked. In particular, how he saw his own work and that of his department in relation to the rest of the functions of the organisation. This was adapted for our purposes in the following way. Departments and functions of the original form were translated into 'jobs' and 'work'. Each participant was asked how he saw other peoples' jobs in relation to his own. A 7-point bipolar scale was again used. There were 4 sheets yielding 4 profiles of other peoples' jobs. Each individual rated the same jobs throughout the evaluation period. By careful balancing, a substantial number of ratings per job function was possible. This allowed more than a gross analysis of the PFI scores. The main purpose of the PFI was to monitor any change in participants' overall view of the work organisation. In addition, it was possible to look at the ways in which people in certain jobs viewed people in other jobs; e.g., how waiters see griddlers.

Customer Measure

Customer perception of service (CPS). The final questionnaire to be described was used to monitor customers' perception of service at the sites that were trained. This was a very simple questionnaire consisting of 12 seven-point bipolar scales, followed by space for additional comments. The poles of these scales were developed from material supplied by HCITB from their assessments of salient customer expectations.

It should be said that it was really beyond the scope and budget of the present project to have made a thorough investigation of customer attitudes to service and this rating sheet does have certain limitations. Nevertheless, it was felt that some attempt should be made to monitor customers' perception of service. A sample of between 200 and 250 was used on each of the two occasions when the CPS was administered; i.e. immediately prior to training and then 12 months after this first administration.

Labour Turnover

Over the 5-month period following training, an account was kept of the number of staff leaving company employment from the various research groups; i.e. those who had undergone training and those who had acted as controls. The host company also generously made available labour turnover figures for the individual motorway sites. Thus, the researchers were able to look at the number of leavers from the reseach groups, as compared to the site figures for comparable periods of the same year and the previous year.

Controls and Comparisons

The trainees in both types of courses were given the same questionnaires, which allowed for the direct comparison of change measures across types of training. In effect, each set of courses became the control for the other. In addition, it was decided to have the trainee act as his own control to check for changes over time. This was particularly easy to do with the perception and some of the behavioural measures. This was achieved by taking two measures prior to training (4 weeks before and just before training) so that later measures (just after and 4–6 months after training) could be compared. The *Bunker* inventory was also administered in a similar fashion. In this way, each trainee was uniquely controlled for a 'training' versus 'no training' effect.

Results

Differences in the Training Programmes as Judged by Content Analysis of Recording Tape

The descriptions of the two training programmes so far have been in terms of anticipated differences in approach. Whether the descriptions are by the researchers or the consultants who designed them, they remain subjective only. That is, no external evidence was provided to indicate that the programmes were truly different.

In order to assess the objective differences, tape recordings were taken of two entire weeks of each training programme and a special rating scale (programme differentiation questionnaire) was devised to help content analyse the recordings. This scale contained ten 9-point bipolar scales which permitted the assessment of the trainer's role (didactic versus unstructured), the amount of structured teaching given, amount of skill instruction given, amount of discussion of group interaction, degree to which participants were directed to attend to ongoing individual and group interaction, and a number of measures of group atmosphere for each type of training programme.

The tapes were divided into 5-minute segments and ten segments were selected randomly for analysis for each training programme. The samples were then placed alternatively on a single tape. Seven independent judges (social scientists) were asked to listen to each sample and then to rate them (without knowledge of what they were listening to) on each of the 10-bipolar scales of the programme differentiation questionnaire. In this way, a large number of assess-

Table I. Judged differences between the two training programmes (from tape recordings)

a) t-test for difference of means

Scale No.	Aspect	'Skills' mean	'Social' mean	Difference of means	Significance
1a	judges' ability to distinguish trainer	6.5714	7.2571	0.6857	t = 0.9780 NS
1b	trainer as teacher	5.8571	2.8000	3.0571	t = 4.264 p < 0.001
2a	discussion of interaction with the group	2.6286	6.5429	3.09143	t = 5.536 p < 0.001
2b	degree of direction to participants to focus on social interaction	2.4571	5.8857	3.4286	t = 4.7805 p < 0.001
3	group feeling in terms of warmth	5.8571	6.4286	0.5715	t = 0.9476 NS
5	instruction through extra-group experience	5.9143	4.7714	1.1429	t = 1.5098 NS (0.05 < p < 0.1)
7	interpersonal trust	6.2571	6.2571	0.0	t = − NS
8	social atmosphere in terms of tension generated	6.3143	5.6286	0.6857	t = 0.9338 NS

0.05 significance level for two-tailed t-test = 2.00.
0.01 significance level for two-tailed t-test = 2.66.
NS = not statistically significant.

b) Using 50 % probability test

Scale No.	Aspect	'Skills' ratings[1]		'Social' ratings[1]		Significance[2]
		1–4	5–9	1–4	5–9	
4	specific skill instruction	11	24	31	3	'social': p < 0.002 'skills': p = 0.05
6	degree of structure in course instruction	10	25	18	15	'social': NS 'skills': p < 0.05

1 Rating scale of 9 points, 1 being low and 9 high; 5 is neutral.
2 50 % p-test used for these scales to avoid the assumption of homogeneity of variance.

ments for each programme were assembled and statistical tests applied to test whether the samples represented two distinctive programmes with respect to the items in the above questionnaire.

The results of this tape analysis show quite clearly that the two programmes do differ in a number of important approaches to training. The 'skills' programme was rated significantly higher than the 'social' programme with respect to (a) amount of skill instruction given, (b) amount of structured instruction given, and (c) the degree to which the trainer adopted a didactic or teaching role (the judges found no difficulty in identifying the trainers of the two programmes). On the other hand, the 'social' programme samples were consistently rated significantly higher than the 'skills' programme on the following items: (a) amount of discussion of group interaction and (b) the degree to which participants were directed to attend to ongoing group interaction. All these results are in keeping with the earlier stated methods and training philosophies of the programmes. It might be noted, in conclusion, that neither of the programmes differed significantly on the 'social atmosphere' scales. Interpersonal trust was equally high for both programmes and, although the 'social' programme was rated as less relaxed than the 'skills' programme, it was also rated as warmer than the other. The differences, however, were not significant.

Results of Evaluation over Time
and between Training Programmes and Controls[2]

Summary of Results

Certain external measures were used to determine training effects besides the set of questionnaires administered to trainees and their work associates. One important external measure is labour turnover. The labour turnover figures for the sites following both of the social skill training programmes, when contrasted to the comparable period in the previous year, indicated a significant reduction (table II). In addition, when the site figures for the period in the year of training are compared with the proportion of *trained* leavers, the site figures are seen to be significantly higher than both trained groups. It should be noted that the figures for the comparison group are also considerably less than the site figures, but higher than the trained groups (table III).

Another external measure the researchers used consisted of data gathered from a survey of customer response to staff service at motorway sites. This data came from the administration of the customer perception of service questionnaire (CPS). The questionnaire was administered in four types of restaurant

2 Due to the large quantity of data generated in this study, a brief review of the main results only will follow. The detailed statistical results will not be included in their entirety to conserve space, but they can be obtained from the senior author.

Table II. Percent reduction in labour turnover for all sites involved in the social skill training programmes (for 5-month period from November to March in 1969/70, as compared to 1970/71)

'Social' programme		'Skills' programme	
site 1	site 2	site 3	site 2
23.2	5.0	17.0	25.0

Table III. Leavers in the trained and untrained groups

	Total of participants	Leavers	Significant difference[1] in comparison with parent site populations
'Skills' courses	60	8 (13.3 %)	$\tau = 2.8892$ $p = 0.002$
'Social' courses	47	5 (10.6 %)	$\tau = 3.1165$ $p = 0.001$
			Significant difference between programme and comparison groups
Comparison group	42	9 (21.4 %)	'skills' versus Cs: $\tau = 1.0797$ $p = 0.14$ 'social' versus Cs: $\tau = 1.3958$ $p = 0.08$

1 Using τ-test for the significance of different proportions.

units, two units 'wholly' trained in either the 'social' or the 'skills' programme, and two units partially trained in either the 'social' or the 'skills' programme. The change over the 12-month period between the two administrations of the CPS was found not to be significant for the partially trained units and for the wholly trained unit of the 'skills' programme. The wholly trained unit of the 'social' programme showed significant positive change on four of the scales (friendly, welcoming, respectful and tactful) directly related to service staff's social skills.

We will now turn to the data generated by questionnaires completed by participants and their associates. The first of these to be considered will be the perceived function questionnaire (PFI). The PFI might be thought of as measuring organisational awareness. In our study, we used this questionnaire to monitor changes in the way people perceived the jobs of their work associates in relation to their own. The 'skills' programme participants showed considerable

Table IV. Changes in Customers Perception of Service (CPS) over 12 months

Position pole of scale	Scale No.	partially trained, using 'social' programme			wholly trained, using 'social' programme			wholly trained, using 'skills' programme			partially trained, using 'skills' programme		
		x^2	sign of change at follow-up	p	x^2	sign of change at follow-up	p	x^2	sign of change at follow-up	p	x^2	sign of change at follow-up	p
Helpful	1	4.28	−	< 0.05	0.52	=	NS	0.56	+	NS	0.56	−	NS
Friendly	2	0.21	+	NS	8.06	+	< 0.01	2.77	+	NS	5.37	−	< 0.05
Efficient	3	2.12	+	NS	0.25	−	NS	0.41	−	NS	1.69	−	NS
Good humoured	4	0.05	−	NS	1.59	+	NS	0.22	−	NS	1.47	−	NS
Speedy	5	0.16	−	NS	0.33	+	NS	0.35	+	NS	0.23	−	NS
Courteous	6	0.18	−	NS	3.74	+	NS	0.49	−	NS	1.67	−	NS
Pleasant	7	0.89	−	NS	0.06	=	NS	0.04	+	NS	1.41	−	NS
Welcoming	8	1.22	−	NS	6.27	+	< 0.02	0.55	−	NS	2.12	−	NS
Hygienic	9	1.17	−	NS	0.13	+	NS	0.61	−	NS	11.01	−	< 0.001
Respectful	10	1.02	−	NS	4.37	+	< 0.05	0.04	+	NS	9.32	−	< 0.01
Anticipating needs	11	0.00	−	NS	0.16	+	NS	0.46	+	NS	0.80	+	NS
Tactful	12	0.07	−	NS	5.03	+	< 0.005	0.14	−	NS	1.93	−	NS
Mean of medians² for sites		5.33			5.91			6.41			3.83		

1 The expression 'partially trained' and 'wholly trained' refers to site *units*. 'Wholly trained' describes units with more than 60 % of their staff trained. 'Partially trained' refers to units with less than 30 % of their staff trained.
2 Median score on 7-point scales of CPS.
NS = not statistically significant.

positive change on only one of the scales of the PFI — 'improving personal relationships of individuals'. The participants of the 'social' programme showed significant positive change on five of the scales. All five scales were connected with cognitive aspects of the trainee's relations with people in different jobs. That is, the trainee improved his 'insight into the other's job', 'knowledge of the job', 'awareness of the problems of the job', 'understanding of job status', and 'thinking about the job'. It does appear that the PFI is pointing up differences in the effects of the two training programmes.

The data from the other behavioural change questionnaire (perceived change inventory, PCI) is not easy to interpret. Comparing the number of persons changed in the trained groups with those of the comparison group at follow-up (3—5 months after training) reveals that a significantly higher number of persons were reported as changed in both programmes. However, when we compared these figures with those for a comparable period to training, none of the groups show significant differences over time. Other comparisons over time show that more work associates reported change for participants of the 'social' programme than for either 'skills' programme participants or members of the comparison group, but the differences were not significant. The confirmed change scores (agreement by two or more work associates on a particular change in the trainee) were also higher for the 'social' programme when compared over time, but again the difference was not significant. Looking separately at programme participants coming from only partially trained units showed that more positive change in his relationship with colleagues and customers was reported by his work associates (after training) for participants of the 'social' programme than for participants of the 'skills' programme. This change was significant at the 0.01 level. In addition to descriptions of change, the PCI gave provision for a rating of behavioural change. The data from this section of the questionnaire reveals the same pattern of results as the descriptive section. Both training programmes show higher ratings after training than before, whereas the comparison group ratings remain relatively stable, but again differences over time are not significant.

One of the problems one meets when using bipolar rating scales is that of skewness in the distribution of the responses. This occurs, for instance, when raters exaggerate their positive responses to scales. This kind of difficulty arose for the researchers when analysing the data of the perceptual questionnaires (changes in perceived image, CPI). In an effort to circumvent this problem, maximum scores were eliminated from the analysis, for, it was argued, these could not show positive change over time. When positive change was examined over time, differences in the training effects of the two programmes were revealed. Participants in the 'social' programme showed significant change on more scales when rating themselves than when rating their ideal work associate. On the other hand, participants of the 'skills' programme changed significantly on more scales of the ideal rating than they did on the self-rating. For both groups, the scales on which significant change occurred were similar for the self-rating and the others rating and the self-rating and the ideal rating. There is also evidence to suggest that for participants on 'social' programme, observers' perception of the participants and the participants' own perceptions of themselves moved closer together over time.

It is interesting to compare the data from the external measures and the questionnaires reviewed so far with the subjective reports of participants themselves. These are contained in the post-course critique questionnaire (PCC) and its associated questionnaire, the inventory of planned change (IPC). An analysis of this material makes it quite clear that the participants of both programmes liked their courses and thought that the courses would help them to carry out their jobs. The participants of the 'social' programme felt that the course had helped them *to understand themselves, to understand other people, to get along better with people* and also *to notice other people's feelings more.* The response that the course had helped participants to understand themselves was found to be significantly above the average response level to this part of the PCC. They did not think that the course would help them to work faster or to give better service to customers. Their responses were significantly below average with respect to the understanding of customers' needs, giving better service to customers, and generally doing a better job. The 'skills' programme participants were generally more positive on this section of the questionnaire. All the items on the check-list were responded to positively and in only two cases was this not significant. It is perhaps more interesting to look at the items which attracted a response that was significantly above the average for the group. Two responses were in this category; the participants thought that the course had helped them to be more confident and to get along better with people at work. Like the participants of the 'social' programme, they did not think the course had helped them to work faster. The response to this latter item was significantly below the average item response. The 'skills' programme participants did not think the course had helped them to understand other people's jobs better and the response to this item again was significantly below the average. Participants of both programmes rated their instructors very highly. They found the instructors very helpful, friendly, effective and clear. Rating the instruction they had received, the response again was highly positive. They thought their instructors had conducted the courses in a highly successful manner. The courses were rated as both good and practical. Participants of the 'skills' programme tended to be more positive on some of these aspects. There was a significant difference in the participants' attitude to the length of the course and, in general, the participants of the 'skills' programme found their courses to be too short. Those trained under the 'social' programme were indifferent on this matter.

The data from the IPC show that participants from both programmes intended to make changes in their behaviour in the light of what they had learned from their courses, when they returned to work. Over 60 % of the participants of both programmes made plans. At follow-up, more participants of the 'social' programme remembered their plans and generally remembered more of them than did participants of the 'skills' programme. At follow-up, the planners felt they had been generally successful in putting their plans into effect. The planners who had taken part in the 'skills' programme gave significantly more positive ratings in this respect. When examining the plans of the participants of the 'social' programme, the researchers found a high correlation between the types of plans listed and the participants' review of main course learning at follow-up approximately five months later. There was no similar correlation in the 'skills' programme data. However, the 'skills' programme participants' review of course learning did correlate highly with the 'social' programme participants' review of learning at follow-up.

Finally, when the participants of the 'skills' programme were asked to describe the main obstacles to the successful implementation of their learning, only a quarter of the group felt the need to list anything whereas half of the 'social' programme participants described obstacles to learning implementation. Both programmes gave the top nomination to pressures of work and lack of staff, but the participants of the 'skills' programme paired this nomination with that of personality difficulties.

Discussion of Results

It would seem appropriate at this stage to re-examine the project's original objectives. The very first question asked was: Is social skill training a feasible proposition within the hotel and catering industry? This question in effect defined the project's first goal. It was noted in the Introduction that one project executed within a limited sample of the parent population could not conclusively prove feasibility. Within the limits imposed by this sample, however, training in social skill has been shown by the researchers to be feasible. Two types of training programmes were organised and executed within the framework of the original training and evaluation programme. Both approaches to social skill training were seen by the site management, the trainees, the host company training staff and the training consultants who administered the courses as having been a practical proposition and in various ways effective.

Closely linked to the first question is the second: Could social skill training be effective if applied to the service staff of the catering industry? There is some evidence to show that training was effective in this context. Perhaps the most interesting is that of labour turnover. For instance, the number of staff leaving who came from the groups that had been trained, was significantly less than those leaving the sites as a whole over the same period. This could be the result, however, of the selection of staff to be trained, that is, staff who were more satisfied with their work and, therefore, less likely to leave may have been sent on the training. This is not very likely, however, in view of the fact that the site managers were restricted in their selection to staff from certain job functions and from certain organisational work groups.

In order to check that we were not dealing with abnormally high site figures, those for the comparable period in the previous year were also examined and found to be even higher. This gave the researchers some confidence that the figures used were quite normal for the sites and their comparison was a reasonable one. In terms of labour turnover, therefore, social skill training may be effective. More work in the area would have to be done, however, to say with any conclusiveness that this type of training reduces labour turnover. It is also interesting to note that, although the untrained comparison group's figure for leavers approaches the current overall site figures, it is still nevertheless lower than these. It may be that asking catering staff to take part in a training course away from the site makes them feel that somebody is interested and concerned (halo phenomenon), which may have the effect of reducing turnover.

Effectiveness is probably best measured by a direct assessment of service in the work situation. This was attempted with the CPS and a good deal of positive evidence of change in customers' assessment was found over time. The unit with more than 60 % of its staff trained under the 'social' programme showed negative change on only one scale of this questionnaire and positive change on 9 of a total of 12 scales. The change on 4 of these scales was statistically significant ($p < 0.05$). The scales in question were 'friendly–unfriendly', 'welcoming–unwelcoming', 'respectful–disrespectful', and 'tactful–tactless'. All these scales are undoubtedly sampling what most people would regard as areas of 'social skill'. The wholly trained unit of the skills programme also shows positive change, although this does not reach a statistically significant level on any of the scales. Once again, however, the scales exhibiting the positive change are distinctly 'social skill' scales. The results of the CPS also seem to show that if training effects are to make any impact on customers, training that does not involve more than 30 % of the staff is unlikely to achieve this objective. Another way of putting this might be to say that no manager can really expect any payoff from social skill training at the customer level until at least half of his staff have completed their training. This is not to say that training of less than 30 % of the staff of a unit does not improve social skills *within* the unit. There is some evidence from the behaviour change questionnaire (PCI) to suggest that even minimal training leads to some improvement in the social relations of the work group in question.

So far we have discussed training effectiveness from the point of view of the customers and the company. In doing do we have also, to some extent, answered the training instructors question of 'what sort of end-product should I expect from a social skill training course?' to speak of social skill training effectiveness, however, means that, at some point, change has occurred in individuals. The types of changes likely to have occurred are changes in perception, changes in intentions and changes in behaviour. There will probably also be changes in individuals' motivation. The majority of our questionnaires were in fact designed to monitor such changes. In turning to discuss these questionnaires, we will continue to look at the effectiveness of training, but also we will be answering further questions such as 'Did the different types of training have different effects?' 'Is one method seen to be preferable to the other?' and later 'How did participants respond to the two methods of training used?'

The results of the behaviour change questionnaire (PCI) present problems of interpretation not only for the reader but also for the researchers. The main difficulty here is to know just how much weight to put on the descriptions of change given prior to training. Most researchers in the past have not taken a change measure prior to training, but have simply compared the post-training measure of change for their training groups with a comparison group. It is because we suspected this procedure that we decided to insert a measure of behavioural change prior to training for all groups. In doing so, we demonstrated what we had suspected to be the case, namely, that different groups in a field situation might have quite different initial levels of response. However, to demonstrate this does not in itself present an explanation of why this might be. Only further research could completely clarify the matter. Yet, in the absence of this, we can put forward some tentative suggestions. Looking at the figures for the comparison group, we can see that 61 % of this group was reported to have changed over the 3-month period prior to training. This is probably in part due to the high rates of turnover in existence at the sites over, at least, the past two years. This means that a substantial number of the staff at the sites will have completed less than 12 months' service with the company. It is not surprising then that quite a lot of change will be going on all the time and what is more, it will be seen to be going on. At this point in time, the comparison group also shared with the training groups the feeling that they were special people, because they had been chosen to take part in our research programme.

It may well be that the respondents had a tendency to exaggerate their assessments of change at this time due to a desire to co-operate fully with the researchers. The training groups, too, were in a similar position, but there may well have been some enhancement of positive responding (on the behavioural change questionnaire), due to the knowledge that they had been chosen to actually go on the courses. When we consider that each training method adopted a different attitude towards pre-training meetings with participants and in their approach to motivating them, it is not surprising that there is some difference on the measure, that is, the ones who had more 'appreciation meetings' and greater motivation prior to training would respond more positively (this was particularly true of the 'skills' course). In fact, when we look back and inspect the number of changed individuals as a percentage of the total in each group, we can see that there is a progressive increase in the proportion of persons reported as changed prior to training as we move from participants of the comparison group to those of the 'social' and those of the 'skills' programme.

However, we would not expect to find this kind of enhancement of change operating at the follow-up period. The training programmes are, at this point in time, a thing of the past, and filling in evaluation forms is a chore rather than a novelty. The figures are very much what one would predict from this line of argument. One would expect that the figures for the two training groups would now be equal to or higher than the change figures found before training but, on the other hand, those for the comparison group should now be less than these groups *before* training. It must be stressed that such an explanation or rather interpretation can only be tentative at this stage. There are alternative explanations which may be equally acceptable. To conclude our comments on the behavioural change questionnaire, with a cautionary note: There is also evidence in the results that the PCI is not a very good indicator of change when used below the level of management. Comments on change in the descriptive sections of the PCI for all groups were always brief and tended toward generalisations about personal character rather than distinct descriptions of change. Also, as the data indicate, a high proportion of the change ratings consisted of neutral 'no change' ratings for all of the groups but particularly so for the group trained under the 'social' programme regime. Behavioural change within the units as measured by the PCI does not in general seem to be as high as one might have hoped..

One of the questionnaires that showed up distinct differences between the trained groups was the PFI. It is important to remember that the scales of the PFI refer to the job being rated and not the job of the individual doing the rating; however, the jobs rated were always related to the trainee's own job. The scales on which the 'social' programme achieves significance all refer to various aspects of *knowledge* about thy other person's job. The PFI results show that after training they had a clearer insight into the way the other person's job affected theirs, they had a better appreciation of the value to the work group of the other's job, they found it easier to understand what the other person's job was all about and, finally, they felt that they had a better understanding of the other person's job generally. On the other hand, only one of the PFI scales showed a change for the 'skills' programme. Participants involved in this training found it easier to get on with people who held the jobs that were being rated. In other words, the participants of the 'social' programme do seem to have a firmer grasp of organisational knowledge after training than the participants of the 'skills' programme. This is not unexpected when one remembers that the 'social' programme deliberately sets out to re-recreate in miniature the work groups that the participants were originally drawn from. However, there is nothing in the PFI results that suggest that the 'social' programme participants went beyond acquiring knowledge of the work organisation. Scales which might have shown the participants as more actively involved in social relations within their work unit were not found to change after training: aspects of job interrelations, communications, contacts between jobs, and the dependence of the participants' job on the job being rated.

.More differences between the programmes emerge when we look at the perception measures on the CPI questionnaire. If the number of scales on which changes are occurring is a reliable indication of perceptional modification, then participants in the 'social' programme appear to be more concerned with the way they see themselves than with the way they see others. The 'skills' trainees, on the other hand, are seen by others as changing on more scales than they see themselves changing on. The significant changes in both cases appear to come from the start of the course and the end of the course, and so it is reasonable to assume that these differences are methodological in origin. They are, in fact, the kinds of difference that anyone with knowledge of the two training methods and their associated philosophies would be led to expect. Put briefly, the 'skills' trainees who have spent the 5 days of their course learning how to improve their repertoire of skills for dealing with others, should be able to put their newly found knowledge into practice when given the opportunity immediately after the course. On the other hand, the 'social' trainees who have spent most of their time in a T-group-type situation throughout their course should have, at the end of it, a new insight into themselves as a result of the feedback they have been receiving in the group. Turning to the long-term effects on perception over time, it would seem that the discrepancy between self-ratings and observer ratings of the self-widened for participants of the 'skills' programme but narrowed for participants of the 'social' programme. This would suggest that by follow-up (3–5 months after training), there was little difference between self-ratings and observer's ratings of the participants of the 'social' programme; in other words, they were better able to see themselves as others saw them.

A practical question that an interested training instructor might very well raise is 'How did the participants respond to each of the programmes they engaged in?' It is a question which the researchers themselves were very much interested in. Some training authorities have argued that forms of social skill training such as T-group training should not be used to train staff below the level of junior management. It has been argued that training would be unsuitable but may indeed be positively harmful to participants. In order to see if these fears were justified, we included a section in the PCC which all participants completed to help discover just what participants thought of the courses and the training instructors. When we asked participants if they had liked the courses, there was an overwhelming positive response. The same kind of positive response was given when we asked the participants if they thought their courses had been effective, except that the participants of the 'skills' programme were even more positive.

The same pattern was followed when questions were asked about the method the instructor had used and the instructor's personality.

The check-list response data, which are also found on the PCC, give further details of how the participants saw the courses as having helped them. Because of the high response rate of the 'skills' trainees to this part of the questionnaire, it was found to be more useful to look at items that had achieved a response rate significantly above the average and to look at differences between the two groups in this respect. We found that both groups had rated their respective courses very highly on 'helping them to notice other people's feelings'; but besides this, the 'social' programme trainees had also rated significantly higher that the course had 'helped them to understand themselves better'. This seems to be clearly in line with the findings of the perception questionnaire that we discussed earlier. 'Skills' programme participants also rated highly 'getting along better with people at work' and 'gaining confidence'. These findings again are in line with those of the perception questionnaire (CPI). The participants of the 'social' programme seemed to have deliberately avoided checking items that referred directly to the service they gave to customers. This is not too surprising, one would not expect participants in a T-group-type of course to relate this training directly to better 'service to customers', although one might expect a positive change in this direction in 'actual behaviour' over time. In fact, it was found 9 months after training that the 'social' programme trainees were seen by customers as having improved their service (CPS).

Again it is not surprising that both groups deliberately avoided responding to the suggestion that the course had helped them to work faster. They were aware that they had participated in a social skills course, not a manual skills course. The participants of the 'skills' programme avoided responding to the suggestion that the course had helped them 'to understand other people's jobs'. This reinforces the view that came out of the work relations questionnaire (PFI) findings that the participants of the 'skills' programme did not see their form of training as having improved their knowledge of the job functions of others and of the work organisation.

The high intention to change revealed by the IPC completed at the end of the course is a typical response of participants who have enjoyed their course and felt they have gained a lot from it. To a large extent it reflects the euphoria that anyone who has participated in a successful training course will recognise and remember. The danger is, of course, that the euphoria may blind the trainee to the realities of the work situation that he will be returning to. The last day of the training course is very important in this respect, because it will be on this day that the trainer must try to build a bridge between the training situation and the work environment. The IPC and its associated follow-up questionnaire (IPCpQ) are constructed primarily to look at this aspect of training. The way this was done was to ask participants 'how co-operative people would be when they returned to work'. They were then questioned further as to how helpful their boss would be, their work associates would be, and finally their subordinates. Their responses were then compared with their ratings of actual cooperation made at the follow-up. It was argued that a large discrepancy would mean that transfer of learning had not been easy, that the difficulties of transfer had been underestimated and, possibly, that the participants had suffered some disillusionment on their return to work. On the other hand, a small discrepancy would indicate a comparatively smooth transfer from the training programme to the work site. Participants of the 'skills' programme showed significant change on three of five of the relevant questions. Participants of the 'social' programme showed significant change on only one of the questions. All the significant changes were due to higher positive values immediately after training. We then looked to see if participants adhered to these outcomes, by correlating 'planned change' *after* training with the *follow-up* period. It was found that the correlation for the participants of the 'skills' programme between the end of course assessment of learning and the follow-up reassessment was very low and not significant. The same correlation for the participants of the 'social' programme is highly significant ($p < 0.01$); that is, the two assessments are seen to be ranked similarly. In addition, the correlation across programmes at follow-up shows again a high correlation ($p < 0.01$), which seems to indicate that the ranking of 'skills' programme is now closer to that of 'social' programme participants. Taken altogether then, both sets of data seem to indicate that participants of the 'social' programme found transfer of learning to the work situation easier and smoother than the people of the 'skills' programme. And, in addition, the 'skills' trainees described at the follow-up period (3–5 months after training) found more of the planned changes on training outcomes than originally expressed by the 'social' trainees immediately after the courses.

A number of obstacles, which trainees of both programmes experienced in the implementation of course learning, were expressed at the follow-up period. Participants of both courses nominated pressure of work and lack of staff as chiefly responsible for obstructing transfer of learning. In addition, participants in the 'skills' programme listed 'personality difficulties' as equally a blockage to learning implementation as the above. By 'personality difficulties' are meant problems created by the participants' personalities and not the personalities of others. Almost a fifth of the obstacles nominated by the 'skills' trainees referred to 'management difficulties'. The 'social' programme participants did not list any management difficulties and all other obstacles besides 'pressure of work and lack of staff' are at or below the response level of 16 %. It is difficult, therefore, to know how much meaning to attach to these ratings.

The trainers' descriptive reports reveal that, though trainers of both programmes thought their courses were not wholly successful, they did believe, nevertheless, that they had achieved a moderate degree of success. The predictions of both trainers as to training outcomes was in the main substantiated by our independent measures. The 'skills' programme trainers believed that their participants would gain in confidence and the ability to 'sell themselves' and show an increased understanding of and sympathy with people generally. In addition, the 'skills' trainees suggested in the PCC that they would get on rather better with people at work, and have more confidence. They also believed they would be more perceptive to other people's feelings. The trainers of the 'social' programme predicted more changes in the trainees' perception than in their behaviour at work. Other outcomes would be an increase in trust, tolerance and the understanding of people. 'Understanding people' and 'tolerance' were referred to as main outcomes by 'social' programme participants, both immediately after the courses and at follow-up.

It is difficult to summarise the large amount of data presented in this report without doing some injustice to the results as they stand. The researchers believe that the main goals of the research have been successfully accomplished. They have shown that both programmes were qualitatively different, that training had a substantial effect on labour turnover figures, and that some impact was made on customers' perception of service. Apart from certain methodological constraints in the behavioural change (PCI) analysis, it was found that there was evidence of behavioural change. The work relations questionnaire and the person perception questionnaire (PFI and CPI, respectively) revealed that some participants after training had learned to see themselves, their associates and the various jobs their associates performed, in a different and more positive light. When we turned our attention to the way participants themselves had responded to the two training methods, it was clear that a majority of participants had enjoyed themselves, found the course helpful, and expressed a desire to modify their behaviour in the light of what they had learned.

References

1   *Argyle, M.:* Social interaction (Methuen, London 1969).
2   *Buchanan, P.C. and Brunstetter, P.H.:* A research approach to management development, part I and II. J. Amer. Soc. Trg. Dir. *12:* 18–27 (1959).
3   *Bunker, D.R.:* Individual applications of laboratory training. J. appl. behav. Sci. *1:* 131–148 (1965).
4   *Campbell, J.P. and Dunnette, M.D.:* Effectiveness of T-group experiences in managerial training and development. Psychol. Bull. *70:* 73–104 (1968).
5   *Cooper, C.L. and Mangham, I.L.:* T-groups: a survey of research (Wiley, London 1971).
6   *Damodaran, L.:* Social skills in the hotel and catering industry. Unpublished manuscript (Brunel University, London 1967).
7   *Harrison, R.:* Cognitive change and participation in a sensitivity training laboratory. J. cons. Psychol. *30:* 517–520 (1966).
8   *Harrison, R.:* Research on human relations training design and interpretation. J. appl. behav. Sci. *7:* 71–86 (1971).

9   *Kelly, G.A.:* The psychology of personal constructs (Norton, New York 1955).

10 *Miles, M.:* Human relations training: processes and outcomes. J. Counsel. Psychol. *7:* 301–306 (1960).

11 *Osgood, C.E.; Suci, G.A., and Tannenbaum, P.H.:* The measurement of meaning (University of Illinois, Illinois 1957).

12 *Pickard, O.G.; Thomas, L.F.; Snapes, A.W., and Clare, J.N.:* Research into training for skills in the hotel and catering industry. Unpublished manuscript (Ealing Technical College, London 1969).

13 *Schein, E.H. and Bennis, W.G.:* Personal and organisational change through group methods (Wiley, New York 1965).

14 *Tannenbaum, R.; Weschler, I.R., and Massarik, F.:* Leadership and organisation (McGraw-Hill, New York 1961).

15 *Valiquet, M.I.:* Individual change in a management development program. J. appl. behav. Sci. *4:* 313–325 (1968).

16 *Vegt, R. van der:* Personal communication regarding ongoing research (Institute of Social Science, University of Utrecht, Utrecht 1970).

17 *Whyte, W.F.:* Human relations in the restaurant industry (McGraw-Hill, New York 1948).

Authors' address: Dr. *Cary L. Cooper* and Mr. *H. Oddie,* Department of Psychology, The University, *Southampton SO9 5NH* (England)

Interpers. Develop. *3:* 40–67 (1972)

Group Training with Students in Higher Education

N. Levine

Department of Psychology, Brunel University, Uxbridge, Middlesex

In order to add another dimension to the educational process, group work has, for the past few years, been used with students in colleges and universities. Whilst most of this development has been in the United States, group work has been used also in Britain and Europe. The focus of this work has been to try to develop methods of education that depend on student participation and to integrate a student's experiences with more formal methods of teaching. Although this development in educational methods has been concentrated at a few centers, it is nevertheless an innovation in teaching methods which is rapidly gaining momentum. In this paper, therefore, I want to discuss the use of group training methods with student populations in institutes of higher education. My focus will be to look at a number of issues that relate specifically to students, and then to show how group work can be utilized around these issues. First, I will discuss the use of T-groups with students, because this has been the major application of group participation methods, and second, to a lesser extent, I will discuss the use of role playing methods as a newer development in participation methods. In all this, I am basing my analysis on my own experiences with student groups over the last ten years, rather than on any 'objective' and empirical methods, and consequently I want to acknowledge the inevitable biases that a subjective analysis gives. Because group work with students varies from one situation to another, I will concentrate more on a number of general issues that are common to students and institutes of higher education.

T-Groups with Students

In one sense, I find it odd to be writing about group training with students. Students are, after all, people like the rest of us and to single them out for discussion somehow creates the illusion that they are really different. I find that T-groups with students are very similar to T-groups with other populations, for the same kinds of issues appear in student groups as in other groups. Nonetheless, there are certain advantages to using group methods within academic settings for students.

First of all, a T-group can be a very good personal learning experience for students. Most students are between 18 and 22 years of age and are usually in the transitional stage preceding adulthood. They are filled with doubt, self-criticism, and are attempting to define themselves. To have a T-group at this age can allow them to test their feelings against others and to try to objectify their ideas about themselves; if all goes well, the effect can be truly therapeutic. Secondly, a T-group is a very good place to learn about how groups operate; if they are incorporated within a course in which such knowledge is useful (e.g. psychology, sociology, social administration), the practical information learned from such groups can clarify and integrate some of the general theoretical ideas that are being examined in the course. If the T-group is accompanied by a set of lectures and role playing sessions about group behavior, the immediate comparison between theoretical ideas and practical experience can lead to a much more insightful and critical understanding of these fields. Thirdly, a T-group can be used to break down the usual passivity of students in learning situations. Most students, with a few exceptions, have been given a very authoritarian secondary education in which they learn — putting it crudely — that truth exists and that this knowledge is invested in the presence of the teacher. The tendency is, therefore, for most students to accept a very passive attitude to learning. When they approach a university or college, they expect to take this passive role in the classroom, and they orient themselves only to doing whatever is necessary to pass their exams and to get their degree. Many higher education institutions further reinforce this attitude by putting their students in a very anonymous situation, with large lectures and the occasional seminar or tutorial where the lecturer may or may not show interest in the students. The effect is to make the undergraduate feel that he is isolated from his teachers and to feel that perhaps the ideas are not worth exploring or criticizing unless required for a degree. While there are institutions in which this structure does not exist, this situation is probably more the rule than the exception. A T-group within such a setting may not be able to compensate fully for the overall effect of the environment, but it can allow the students to feel a little closer to at least one staff member and make them feel a little more identified with their department.

T-Groups versus Group Therapy

For personal growth, T-groups can be used to help student adjustment through greater understanding and self-awareness. I should point out, however, that in no way should T-group work be seen as formal psychotherapy, replacing other methods of helping and consultation. T-groups have a limited purpose and scope and are not *therapy* as such. While attendance at a T-group can be therapeutic for an individual (i.e. he learns something about himself), the main goal is primarily educational. Individuals attending a T-group do so in order to learn about themselves, how they affect other people, and how groups work. They do not come in order to gain help about specific problems nor to have some problem cured. I mention this because there is considerable confusion about the functions of T-groups. The T-group movement has been aimed mostly at education and has developed its techniques and orientation around this aim. Most T-group trainers are in substantial agreement about this and most are careful not to create expectations that they are providing therapy. What makes T-groups appear to be group therapy is the heavy dependence on emotional expression in the situation. T-groups thrive on emotion; participants spend their time discussing how people feel about each other, how people treat each other, what impact certain persons have on others, and so forth. Most forms of group therapy also utilize such behavior (see, for example, 31), but the emphasis is different. In group therapy, the participant is (1) a 'patient' (2) who has come in order to help himself and (3) is usually under the auspices of a therapist. The therapist is an individual who is trained to help people, who sees his role in the group as that of helping individuals. In the T-group, on the other hand, the participant is (1) a member (2) who has come in order to learn about group behavior and about his behavior in a group situation, and (3) he comes under his own initiative or the initiative of an institution (e.g., his job, university). The trainer sees himself as helping the group, rather than the individuals, to develop. Thus, there are different expectations on the part of both the participants and the leader in T-groups than there are in therapy groups, and the effect of these expectations is to limit the intensity of personal exploration in the groups. There is a concentration on the 'here-and-now', rather than on the reasons that individuals have developed in the way they have.

It is, of course, not possible to draw a sharp distinction between what is happening 'here-and-now' and the expectations, feelings, assumptions, and life history that participants bring into the group (i.e. their personality). Why people do various things in groups obviously must reflect their personalities. The difference is one of emphasis. The participants, when they enter the group, bring bits and pieces of 'out there' into the discussion to share with others. But as the group develops, there is a shift towards topics relating to 'in here' (19); the group becomes inward-looking after a while. Nevertheless, the feelings and thoughts from 'out there' affect the way the group initially begins, and it also has an effect on the way people end the group and prepare to go back to their regular social situations. Therefore, the types of anxieties that students have concerning their place in the college or university will come up inside the group and will affect the types of behavior that occur. By looking at the types of actions expressed in the group and the effects of these actions on others, students can learn something about what others feel about the institution, as well as learning about group behavior and their own impact in the group. In this way, T-groups can be useful in aiding individual adjustment into the institution and giving students a chance to look at their feelings in the context of a supportive, enquiring atmosphere. In order to see this, however, it might be useful to discuss briefly the aims of T-groups in general and then see how student groups differ from groups in other social contexts.

Aims in T-Groups

I like to think of T-groups as having four aims, which are really process areas of behavior – the types of behaviors that individuals express: *involvement, interdependency, development of awareness,* and *orientation to the institutional environment.* These aims constitute what most T-groups do (16).

Involvement. Probably the basic issue confronting any group of participants in a T-group concerns individuals getting involved in the situation and making the group develop as a group. Involvement (or lack of involvement) is experienced both as a social experience and as an individual one. Socially, it means that people talk to each other, listen to each other, express feelings (both positive and negative) towards each other, and integrate all the members of the group. Lack of involvement means the opposite: members do not talk to each other, do not listen to each other, do not express feelings towards each other, and do not all participate. Individually, it consists of feelings of warmth and intimacy, feelings of trust towards others, feelings of safety and acceptance, or else the opposite of these feelings (for lack of involvement). Involvement is a primitive social experience which exists in all social situations, and much of what a T-group does revolves around individuals finding a satisfactory level of involvement. In a T-group, involvement is negotiated. The group does not start off with all individuals integrated and talking to each other. Instead, the members are liable to feel the opposite; they do not trust each other and they do not feel safe with each other. The conscious awareness of the situation requires that individuals look at their degree of involvement. Part of their learning is to realize that involvement is essential for other learning to occur. This is often expressed in clichés:

'If you don't get involved, nothing happens.'

'You get out of this situation what you put into it.'

'Why do people just sit here not talking? If you don't talk, we don't know what you are feeling.'

To get involved requires that individuals are willing to take risks, to commit themselves to the situation in the hope of improving the group. Some individuals can get involved more easily than others, obviously, but much of the scope for learning is in this direction. The limits of involvement are so great that few people have ever come close to them, or at best for only moments. For many persons, their own behavior is such that they restrict their own involvement even though it is an unsatisfactory state of affairs.

Alternatively, other individuals get involved without testing limits. They trust other people unquestionably (or unconsciously, they are afraid to *not* trust others). They then find that others do not trust them to the extent that they express, and they get hurt. These people, then, can learn that they can withhold trust towards others until they are sure that they are safe. In a T-group, members can become aware that the negotiation of trust towards others is a process. Additionally, they can learn to explore different levels of trust.

Interdependency. A second focus of T-groups is the establishment of inter-dependency. In order to develop as a group, individuals have to learn to co-operate with each other. But in order to be able to cooperate, they have to develop ways of making decisions. Therefore, some of what goes on in T-groups concerns the negotiation of power and leadership. Most people, in fact, take decision-making and power for granted, for their experiences are in institutional structures where there are often explicit rules about who-has-power-over-whom ('He's the teacher', 'He's my boss', 'He's my subordinate', etc.). But in a T-group, power is not given. Assumptions are made about leadership in the group, but when tested often fall apart. The trainer, for example, is often assumed to be the leader. But when the trainer fails to provide the necessary leadership, the members learn that they have to take control over the group themselves. This process may take anywhere from five minutes up to the end of the group's history; populations differ as to how quickly they question the assumption of 'trainer as leader'. Students generally do not get too bothered by this assumption. The ambiguous atmosphere of the college or university has made them learn to cope with unclear structure as compared with, say, managers, who work in a more structured environment. However, after the trainer issue has been dealt with, other decision-making structures will assert themselves. Sometimes, a couple of members will dominate the group, with the rest of the members following passively.

A: 'Why don't we do ...?'

B: 'Good. That's an idea. I'll follow.'

A: 'Good. Now we're agreed. We finally made a decision.' (Everyone else — silence.)

Or else, the group may structure itself into a 'noisy group' and a 'quiet group'. The types of communication and decision-making structures that groups adopt will vary, but often they emerge out of assumptions made early in the group's history when members' needs were different. A and B may have come to dominate the group because in the first few meetings, they were the only ones brave enough to talk. Quiet members who initially felt secure when A and B were talking now find that they are trapped in their role and cannot get out. Only by consciously becoming aware of how the group is operating and communicating this to other, can members change the structure and make the group more mutual and interdependent. Therefore, some of the learning that goes on in T-groups concerns becoming aware of group structure and learning to be more flexible.

Development of awareness. Another basic theme in a T-group involves becoming aware of one's impact on other people, other's impact on self, and communicating this awareness to others (feedback). This is very much an individual issue, for rarely in other social situations do people honestly express towards others how they see them (unless they are angry at them, or in love, or in some intense emotional state). But in a T-group, such interactions are basic to the process. People come to a T-group in the hope that they will learn something about themselves. They may want to find out how others perceive them, or about what impact they will have on the group, or even about what the 'expert' (i.e. the trainer) thinks about them. But as with the other aims, participants find that answers to these questions are not ready made. Without involvement, there can be few impressions that others have, or at best relatively superficial impressions. Only with interaction and involvement can meaningful relationships be formed so that useful feedback can occur, and this process, like the others, must be negotiated. Without trust of others, statements made by them will probably have little effect; they will be rejected. Even if there is trust, in fact, feedback may not develop, unless it is encouraged or asked for by others. Members may decide that they do not want to know what others feel, or that other issues are more important. If they decide to give feedback to each other, it may take many forms. The group may ritualize the process by 'going around in a circle'. Or they may take individuals one at a time. Or it may be less structured and may develop slowly. Or it may occur sometimes, but not others. Feedback and awareness are not fixed behaviors; they occur in different ways in different situations. T-groups can become aware of feedback as a process and can explore the consequences of doing it one way or another. Some of the learning that develops concerns not only how people see each other, but the uses of feedback and even the types of feedback that exist (e.g. nonverbal feedback).

Orientation to the institutional environment. A fourth goal that can develop in a T-group concerns the participants relation to their outside environment, whether work or social environment. While this is not a necessary aim of a group – the members may decide not to talk about work – it is an aim that many groups explore. 'What is the environment that we come from? And what can we do when we get back there?' The articles in this book are examining this aim by exploring group work within different environments. For students, the college or university is both a work and a social environment, and they bring into the group aspects of that environment and then, hopefully, take aspects of the group experience back out. It is useful and important not to ignore the work and social environment of the participants but to strike a workable balance between the inward-orientation of the T-group and the external structure of the institution. If the group is to have any use, then what it learned in the group must have some relation to the external world. In the early days of group work, such an orientation was considered unnecessary. It was assumed that people are very conscious of their external environments, but much less of the 'internal' ones – the feelings and assumptions that people make in relation to each other. T-groups became, then, very inward-looking and rejected an external orientation. 'Why are we talking about out there, when such and such is happening right here?' This led to what has been called 'the one-shot T-group'. The T-group trainer, who is an outsider, comes into the institution and 'does his thing'. He then leaves and assumes that what was created in the group will somehow magically work its way into the environment. Fortunately, this orientation is changing, as T-group trainers become more aware of the need to relate T-group process to external structure.

With students, the institutional environment is very much related to the workings of a T-group. The T-group usually takes place within the institution. The members of the group have seen or known each other before and will continue to see each other afterwards. The group, therefore, involves only one part of a relationship that members have towards each other. The institution is an over-riding concern within the group. A number of the assumptions that members make towards each other and even towards the trainer (if he is a teacher in the institution) will have been created outside the group. So, for example, if the trainer is a teacher in the college or university, the participants will not easily ignore this factor and will think of their relationships with the trainer inside the group as having possible consequences outside again. The members will not forget that the trainer is a 'power figure' in the institution and later may have to evaluate the students. While this does not create an impossible barrier, it nonetheless creates a problem that must be discussed or resolved in a way that does not inhibit future growth of the group. Similarly, members of the group may hesitate to reveal their feelings towards other members for fear that these feelings may create an unsatisfactory relationship outside the group. These fears must be explored if the group is to develop. If there is one factor which comes up over and over again in student T-groups, it is this concern about the effect of the group on the members' relationships once outside the group.

Students and the Institutional Environment

The type of institution in which students participate – the college or university – and the relationships that students have towards that institution make T-groups in such contexts different from other T-groups. First, a student remains in a college or university for a temporary period, rather than on a permanent basis. He has come to study for a few years and will leave after this study is completed. His role commitment, therefore, is to himself, rather than to the institution. Thus, a T-group run with students is going to have different implications for the institution than with T-groups run for staff, who have a relatively permanent and long-term relationship with the college or university. Second, students occupy a special position, protected from the demands made by the society for work and self-maintenance. In very few cases do students have to work to support themselves, for they are financed by a grant, parents, or by personal savings. While many students do not live at a very high standard of living, the time spent for study creates a sort of moratorium period for earning their living and this allows them to be more independent in their views and less concerned with the consequences of their actions for the institution. Consequently, T-groups with students tend to be more personally-oriented than T-groups run in other contexts.

Third, because students are usually young and because they are in a transitional position economically and socially, they tend to be less clear and definite about their self-identity. While this lack of clarity creates an emotional uneasiness – on which I shall elaborate shortly – it does mean that students tend to be more flexible in their demands and feel much less threatened when confronted with an ambiguous social situation, such as a T-group. This flexibility, even if superficial, encourages exploration of themes and issues which other populations tend to ignore. There is a 'wait-and-see' attitude with students when confronted by the prospect of a T-group experience, and they feel less threatened by the lack of structure and apparent purposelessness of T-groups about which other populations often complain. Fourth, because of the high value placed on intellectual work in a college or university, students are more able to intellectualize their feelings. They will try to explain events, feelings, and relationships in verbal terms with relative ease and will often do so before working through these issues in an emotional way. T-groups run with students, therefore, tend to be quite intellectual and verbal and have a high work rate. Although a high degree of intellectualization is not peculiar to student groups only, it is a common characteristic of them.

Finally, as a socioeconomic group, students represent a relatively privileged group in society. Most students come from middle and upper class backgrounds. In Britain, for example, only a minority of students come from working class backgrounds (about 25 %) and the proportion of working class students in the universities has not changed in 50 years. Students represent a potentially viable economic group after they graduate. Even though graduate unemployment is increasing, the job prospects for graduates are still much better than for persons without a higher education degree. Therefore, students, in coming to a T-group, are in general less concerned about their future job possibilities and more concerned with their own personal growth. There is a moratorium on economic concerns which allows them to explore their own personal potentialities more easily.

Because of these differences between students and the institutional context within which they work and the institutional context for other populations, many of the issues that emerge in student T-groups are peculiar to the special position of students in society. At the risk of eliciting horrific cries of dissent, let me overgeneralize a little and try to typify some of the issues that are common among student populations and which arise in student T-groups. I do not mean to categorize all students as the same nor to insist that students are always like this. Nonetheless, there are certain themes that constitute student culture, especially in Britain, and which will often develop within T-groups in which students are participants. There are, for instance, strong pressures towards seeking 'freedom' and 'liberation' within student circles. Students feel that they want to explore themselves with the aim of unfreezing and bringing out their hidden resources. They feel that they want to avoid being defined in any restrictive way ('We come here to get away from society. What do you want to bring it in here for?'). There are strong expressions of individuality, with frequently underlying tones of elitism. It is as if they are saying 'I'm free. I'm an individual. Don't try to shackle me. The world is rotten and I don't want to have to conform to it. So, I come here to learn about myself, not to learn about anything about "out there".'[1] And, of course, these feelings of individualism and freedom make students ideal participants for a T-group. They are less rigid, in general, than other groups, more curious about new experiences, and more flexible about trying new things out. On the other hand, they are less realistic about themselves and about the world they live in. Most students feel a need to learn about themselves and to explore their situation. As most of the students are young, their attendance at an institution of higher education represents an intermediate stage between school and adulthood, and one that has the roots of many anxieties and problems.

1 For example, when I asked two classes of social science students at Brunel University, in a questionaire, 'What is the purpose of a University?', approximately 90 % mentioned at least one individual purpose whereas only 30 % mentioned at least one social purpose. At the Middle East Technical University in Ankara, Turkey, there is a more conscious social orientation among the students. When this question was asked in 1969, only 45 % mentioned at least one individual purpose whereas 70 % mentioned at least one social purpose. In an underdeveloped country, a university degree is seen in social and political terms and not just in terms of personal career choice.

Ambiguity and Purposelessness

First, many students experience a higher education institution in an alien-ated way, at least initially. They feel isolated and alone, especially if they have come straight from home without ever having lived by themselves. The institu-tion appears to them emotionally neutral and ambiguous. While other people seem to know what they are doing, for the newcomer the structure of the college or university appears vague and unexplicit. On the one hand, there are some specific norms: classes, appointments with lecturers, certain formal activi-ties. But on the other hand, a large segment of a day is left unstructured and without 'things to do'. Thus, for many students, there is a lack of a purposeful and viable environment, and the experience of this is one of alienation and purposelessness. I remember particularly one friend who used to wander around from coffee bar to coffee bar within the university. So I asked him one day:
   'What are you looking for when you come in here again and again?'
   'Just looking.'
   'But, looking for whom?'
   'Don't know. Just looking.'
   'Anyone in particular?'
   'No. But if I see her I'll let you know.'
   'Are you sure it's a Her? Isn't that an assumption?'
   'Could be, but let me work that one through first.'
   I have heard variations of that conversation a dozen times or more, very much like the theme of *Becket*'s 'Waiting for Godot' (3).
   Given the ambiguous environment of a college or university, students cope with it by creating structure. They organize themselves and their organization itself becomes 'structure and purpose' and only by relating to this self-made structure can the neutrality of the institution be handled. Nonetheless, the pro-cess of creating a viable situation out of nothing is one of the biggest problems for students, even for those who have been around for several years. The process itself is often of a very practical nature, concerning specific problems (e.g., 'What do I do?', 'How can I meet friends?', 'How do I get a girl (boy) friend?', 'What groups do I belong to?', 'What impact can I have on anything?'), but the mani-festations of the problems are emotional and in need of working through. Creat-ing solutions to practical problems, often with few guidelines, creates tensions and frustrations which need to be talked through and understood.

Independence and Identity Confusion

Second, many students suffer what *Erikson* has called 'identity diffusion' (9). These students experience stress in a university or college about their ability to cope with the demands being placed on them, and this often occurs fairly early in their stay at the institution, in the first or second year. Before coming to the college or university, these students have experienced a number of emotional conflicts which they have kept controlled, but in the relatively permissive atmosphere of the college, these conflicts are elicited. The main conflict has to do with a student's sense of independence versus dependence where he becomes aware that he is now responsible for his actions to a much greater extent than before. For young students especially, the protective atmosphere of the home and the school system has limited the amount of independence that they have experienced. Suddenly, a student comes into an institute of higher education and he finds that no one really cares whether he studies that much, where he is only checked upon by his tutor every six months or so, where he finds that teachers will not force him to go to classes, but in the end he is required to pass a series of exams. If he has never lived away from home, the problem of achieving independence then becomes even more acute. On top of this, most students have been pushed fairly hard by their parents and peers in terms of succeeding in the school system. In order to weave their way through the secondary schools and get into a college or university, most students have had to compete fairly intensely and have had to discipline themselves fairly diligently. But in accepting the aspirations of his parents and accepting the required discipline, a student may resent these expectations and competitive urges and may feel that he has been 'manipulated', 'twisted', or even 'determined' by the pressures of others, and the frustrations and resentments may remain within him, smoldering but unresolved. Consequently, when a student comes into the ambiguous structure of the college or university, the day-to-day freedom acts as a sort of trigger which releases these frustrations and angers. The student then initially experiences a fear of not being able to cope with the requirements of the course. These feelings may then turn into feelings of not wanting to cope with the course, or feelings of inadequacy and confusion, and maybe even anger at the course or the institution, which suddenly is seen as being responsible for the feelings of confusion. While students differ a great amount about how much confusion they experience or how they express it, most students have to resolve problems of achieving independence, adopting new roles, and reconciling previous expectations of themselves with their present situation.

Incompatible Educational Norms

Third, many students experience problems of role clarification and become confused about confirming their sense of social reality. A college or university serves a number of functions for the student and a student entering the institution will make certain assumptions about what it is supposed to be. However, he will then find that there are certain incompatibilities between these assumptions. On the one hand, there are public beliefs about what a university or college represents and about its relationship to the society. It is a center of information, with library facilities, computer facilities, and so forth. At the same time, it may be a community cultural center, presenting films, plays and music, which people from the local area may attend. It is also an institution for creating knowledge and communicating that knowledge to the society. Most important for the student, however, is that the institution is a place for training people for specialized, technical, and middle-class jobs. Therefore, the student will be comparing himself with these functions. Is he studying for a particular career? And, if so, what kind of a career does he want? Is he expected to help produce knowledge and how can he help distribute that knowledge to others? The social functions of a higher education institution create expectations about his social role and also create anxieties about what he intends to do after he graduates.

On the other hand, strong pressures within the institution work against such assumptions and generate a sort of counter-culture of beliefs. For example, the university is seen as a place for learning about subjects and ideas, independent of any social use they may have. For the student, who may have gone to college in order to learn something, the question of career is vague and ill-defined in his mind. At the same time, the university or college is seen as a place to develop individual resources and an understanding of oneself. The student may feel that he is attending the institution in order to learn about himself and in order to develop himself in a way almost contrary to what society expects of him. He may feel that he does not want to be pushed into a particular occupation, nor forced to fulfill social expectations. But these latter beliefs will contradict with the first set within the student milieu and the individual student will perceive these as a conflict of expectations.

The problem then becomes one of sorting out these assumptions and finding a proper perspective on them. Other students will hold conflicting viewpoints and may themselves not have worked out their beliefs about higher education. These norms will then clash within the individual and the result will be to create anxiety. He will not know what to believe and may experience confusion and a sense of normlessness. There then develops a need to try to explain his purposes in attending the institution in order to study and this may often take the form of questioning his 'purpose in life'.

Thus, many aspects of student culture can be seen as partly a response to the conflicts. I say partly because types of student culture are usually imported from the outside society and reflect aspects of that society. Consequently, one cannot explain student culture as merely some kind of psychological defense mechanism. However, there is an overlap between the social themes that a particular subgroup represents and the needs that a student experiences in that group. For example, the sense of identity confusion that occurs among some students is one such response, especially among social science students. 'I don't know who I am anymore. I'm not sure of anything. I used to know, but then I started questioning things and now I don't believe in anything.' Other students handle this problem by role modeling, finding an identifiable theme or person and then adopting many of the characteristics of that theme. So, in student culture these days, we have the 'long-hair culture', the 'pop culture', the 'hippy culture', the 'revolutionary culture(s)', the 'Jesus freaks culture', the 'straight culture', and so forth. Each of these cultures, in part, expresses solutions to a perceived incompatibility between goals of education, though they relate in more general ways to different ideologies and have different implications for society. Other students may directly confront the inconsistencies and may try to change the system, against all odds, either individually or collectively. On an individual level, there have been defacings of college property, the creation of paintings and slogans across college walls, and the spontaneous transformations of college property into pop art, while on a more collective level, there have been student demonstrations, occupations, exam boycotts, and other such activities of the student movement. More traditionally, there were the rag weeks and student pranks in Britain and Europe, all of which symbolized the turning upside-down of norms and rules. The formal political and debating groups represented an acceptance of the social purposes of the university and the student's role in going into the society, while there has been the rejection of this social orientation in the beliefs of some students concerning the lack of attention that teachers are supposed to show towards students. 'Teachers don't understand students. Teachers are only interested in their research, not in teaching. Teachers should try to learn from students occasionally.' Of course, teachers will vehemently deny such allegations. 'There is absolutely no truth whatsoever in the claim that teachers are uninterested in their students. We really care about students.' Considering that lecturing loads for college and university personnel is lower than for most other professions, such attitudes are really only counterparts to the inconsistencies in beliefs about higher education. But that is another matter.

On a structural level – on the level of belief and discussion occurring throughout the academic community and relating to the outside society – there are certain long-standing conflicts in education which act themselves out within the student environment. It is not really surprising, then, that students will also come to experience these conflicts and will find that the relative permissiveness of the institution comes up against the social expectations they have of the institution, and this becomes expressed through a continual sense of student dissatisfaction. While these conflicts will take years to work themselves through on a societal level, for the student they become a personal issue and one in need of some resolution at an individual level.

By participating in T-groups, many of the anxieties that students feel can be explored, allowing individuals to examine their own feelings, understand how others are feeling, receive social support for their own feelings, and perhaps come to a better sense of the conflicts of 'out there'. A T-group can be useful in removing a sense of isolation for many students. By talking about their feelings, they achieve a sense of solidarity and empathy with others. A number of students from groups of mine have expressed this by saying that they came to the group (a weekly group, at the time) in order to meet people. Some felt that after they had made some friends, they did not need the T-group anymore; others stayed because they found other needs being satisfied in the group. Still, the sense of isolation that students feel, especially entering students, is itself enough to motivate a student to want to attend a T-group. While it seems a slightly elaborate way of introducing students to each other, it is perhaps a poignant comment on the lack of effectiveness of many of the 'normal' ways of meeting people (e.g., parties, sherry gatherings, mass assemblies). One should not underestimate the importance of meeting people, as a social need. It is a very simple need, but one that is not nearly enough satisfied for many people.

T-groups are capable of satisfying other needs for students, however. They can, for instance, broaden students' sense of competence and remove feelings of helplessness. Many students are shy and feel unable to speak in group situations (e.g., seminars). A T-group can help them try to become more involved. Other students talk too much and tend to dominate situations. A T-group can allow them to get some feedback from others about their impact on the others. Some students find it difficult to talk about their feelings, whilst others find it difficult to listen to other people's feelings. There are a large number of small social behaviors that individuals in a group will generate together, some of which are useful for the individuals concerned, while others are ineffective and create anxiety in the individual. By focusing on what happens in the group, the individuals can look at their behavior and learn something of their impact on other people. The effect of this will be to increase an individual's feelings of effectiveness and competence. And if the other individuals in the group are also part of the work environment (which they are for student T-groups), then this increased sense of competence should carry over into the regular student environment.

More related to the student environment, the members of a student T-group will tend to talk about the institution and share their feelings and perceptions with each other. The difference between discussing the institution within a T-group compared to outside the group (e.g., over coffee) is that the 'here and now' focus of the T-group is going to feed into the discussion and will tend to sharpen the discussion or present it in another light. I have listened to a number of student groups where individuals came into the group complaining about the institution and about the inability of their being able to do anything, and end up by leaving the group talking about the things they felt they could do, often quite unrelated to what they were complaining about initially. The effect of the group was to clarify the problems being presented and take it down to the individual feeling level, and then re-orient the student in the direction that his needs were expressing. For example, a number of students feel that social science is a useless subject to learn. One student put it: 'The capitalist structure does not allow social scientists to adequately do anything. They must channel their energies in the direction consistent with the power structure. If they question the "establishment", they will lose their jobs.' After about three meetings in which he protested about social science, it turned out he really wanted to be a social scientist. 'It sounds like a cushy job. Good hours. Reasonable pay. A chance to be quite creative.' In the end, he was at least willing to openly accept that he wanted to be an academic. He still felt that the capitalist structure inhibited revolutionary actions, but he was more oriented towards trying to cope with the system and try to 'slide through it', being political as he went along. The effect of the group was to help him to discuss the incompatible demands that he was expressing (i.e. 'that useful social science was not possible in a capitalist society', and the fact that he was 'studying for a social science degree in a university'). This does not mean that students will work through their problems or have them shown to be really irrational. The conflicts exist in society and they cannot be explained away. But what a T-group can do is clarify what students feel about the various pressures affecting them, share their perceptions and feelings with each other, and perhaps come to a better perspective of the issues, if only to accept the existence of a conflict.

Methods of T-Group Work with Students

The manner in which groups are run does not, I think, matter very much. For years, I ran weekly groups with the members meeting for an hour or two at a time. More recently, I have been running more concentrated one-, two-, or three-day groups with the members meeting all day. Basically, I cannot see that there are relative advantages of one method over the other. The weekly groups take longer to develop and are less emotionally intense than the concentrated groups, but members are more able to integrate the group with their everyday lives in the weekly group. The concentrated groups give the students an intense, emotional experience while the weekly groups give the students a better perspective on themselves. If one's purpose is to help students to adjust better to their lives, then a weekly group would probably be better, whereas a more concentrated experience gives members a much better awareness of the depth and complexity of emotional life. In fact, during the times I was running weekly groups several years ago, I took to providing an all-night Marathon group for the members after they had met in their weekly groups for about half their meetings. The effect of this was to generate an intense emotional experience and I found that this fed back into the weekly meetings and actually helped the weekly group along.

Because of students' flexibility and greater freedom in time demands, a large range of possibilities are open for planning student groups. Most student participants are interested in self-exploration and are willing to try whatever possibilities are created. In this sense, all the 'tools' of the trade can be used and can be useful: nonverbal exercises, role playing, encounter techniques, fantasy games, intergroup experiences and, even, community groups. Each formal exercise or structure creates something in the groups, and students find whatever happens quite interesting to follow. Compared to other organizational environments (e.g., managers in an organization, social services), an academic environment allows a great degree of freedom to explore any particular issue. Since there is no specific organizational goal to be had from T-groups in an academic community, anything that develops in a T-group is acceptable. This gives student T-groups a slightly paradoxical position in the institution. While the institution exists as an overriding theme within the groups, the group nonetheless has no specific institutional purpose to meet. The students see it as a personal learning experience and not as a situation for learning to change the institution (though this may develop as a by-product of the group).

Further, there are certain advantages to running student groups, compared with other types of organizational settings. First, the relative permanency of the community allows individuals to utilize the group experience more effectively. Feelings and feedback generated in the groups will extend back into the community and will give members a yardstick by which to measure their growth. They can talk about their experiences in the group with the other members later on and can refer back to the group experience whenever they need to do so. This possibility is extremely important for participants. Many times, members of T-groups will experience feelings in the group that they are not able to express at the time, or even clarify to themselves. Yet, after the group is over, when the other members are gone, the individual experiences these feelings suddenly but then finds that he is not able to talk about them to anyone. He then becomes depressed. In fact, this is a very common occurrence for members of T-groups, to have an 'after' depression up to two or three days after leaving a T-group. The existence of a permanent community, however, allows the members to seek out each other and talk about what they are feeling, but were unable to express at the time. This allows a more continual working through of their feelings and encourages a more thorough integration of the group experience into their lives.

Second, the T-group in an academic setting can be useful in aiding improvement in formal teaching situations. I am thinking particularly of seminars, where students who were previously quiet can participate more after a T-group experience, especially if there are others in the seminar who were also in the T-group.

While this is not an essential prerequisite of effective seminar work, T-groups may, nevertheless, have an indirect feedback into the formal structure of the college or university.

At the same time, there are certain difficulties with running student T-groups. The basic one is the problem of authority within the institution. If the trainer is also a teacher in the institution, which I have been when I have run student T-groups, there is the possibility of a role conflict for both the teacher and the students. Both may fear that the group may bias the teacher's ability to fairly evaluate students later on during examinations. They may also fear that the trainer will not be treated as a person in the group, but will remain just a teacher in the eyes of the members. Similarly, the students may feel that the T-group could be unethical if feelings are generated which could later bias the teacher's evaluation of the students on a formal requirement. This is a primitive fear, but it does exist and takes the form of 'If I am criticized in the group by others, or shown to be inadequate or helpless, will this not influence him (i.e. the trainer/teacher) to think of me as weak and ineffectual?'. There are a number of possible role conflicts that could develop inside the group which could not only disturb the group and prevent it from growing, but could have consequences for the members outside the group in the community. There are other ethical issues, as well. If members of the group are expected to be open with each other, then they are bound to gossip about other people, both staff and students, who are not in the T-group. If those other people happen to be friends or colleagues of the T-group participants, then there are conflicts about loyalties and responsibilities towards the T-group members. Similarly, other people in the community, both staff and students, may fear the consequences of a T-group, even though they do not belong to it. A number of staff colleagues have in times past expressed this by saying 'I don't want students discussing me to you in those groups.' Other staff may distrust the groups for other reasons and may talk to students about 'those useless groups'. The students may then be put into a conflict about their loyalties in the situation. There are a large number of possible conflicts that could develop by running a T-group within an academic community with one of the staff members as the trainer.

These problems are not insurmountable, but they must be considered. To think of the group as a closed system is naive, and a staff trainer must be prepared to face a number of difficulties that could develop as the result of setting such T-groups. There are no clear-cut solutions on how to solve these difficulties, but I have found a number of things are useful to do. First, it is essential for the trainer to talk over his expectations of the group with the students *before* the group begins. And it is essential to spell out as clearly as possible what some of the problems could be. In this way, there are fewer ambiguities about what the group represents to the members and to the staff trainer. Second, it is important not to make participation in the group compulsory. T-groups with students should be voluntary and should be seen to be voluntary. If a student is required to attend a T-group, either where a grade is given or not, or where a formal course (e.g., a seminar) is turned into a T-group, then the effect of this could place students in a double-bind situation. A student may not want to participate in this type of situation, but may fear the consequences of not participating. He then will feel that whatever he says has been pulled out of him and he may feel that he was manipulated and exploited. The consequences of this experience are far worse than if special groups were set up and students were invited to attend. Thirdly, it is useful if the staff trainer talks over his feelings and expectations of the group continually as it goes along. In this way, he makes himself part of the group and does not set himself outside it as an 'expert', allowing himself to be seen as a punitive power figure. Only by expressing honesty can a staff trainer overcome the possible role conflicts that could develop in a student T-group. Finally, it is important for a staff trainer to talk over the existence of the group with other staff members and to be aware of what effect the group is having on the other staff members. While he should respect the confidentiality of the material discussed inside the group, he must be sensitive to the conflicts that could be placed on other staff members. It is very much a practical, political exercise trying to run a T-group within a context where other staff may be suspicious and, possibly, threatened. I have found at times that I have even had to invite other staff members to attend the groups in order to demonstrate that the groups are an open exercise in self-awareness and not a secret group designed to undermine the structure of the university. To put it mildly, social tact is very essential.

Group Training as a Method for Learning about Social Reality

Up to this point, the role of group training as a method of self-exploration for students has been considered. There are, however, other uses of group work with students that can be utilized within an academic setting and I will briefly discuss some of these. Aside from self-learning, one advantage of using such methods in a college or university is that they can provide a social experience which can form the basis for intellectual learning. In other words, group training can be used as a method of teaching, especially with respect to social science students, psychology students, social workers, and social service students. Group training methods can be used either by themselves or in conjunction with other teaching methods. Basically, I see four types of group training methods which are useful in teaching: T-groups, role playing, gaming, and simulation. In all these cases, active participation in a social situation is an essential part of the learning process, in contrast to the more passive lecture and seminar methods which are traditional within higher education.

T-Groups as a Teaching Method

In the previous discussion, T-groups as a method for self-exploration were discussed. However, T-groups can also be used as a way for learning about group behavior. They can, for instance, be attached to a formal course in social psychology or group dynamics (assuming that participants have volunteered to go to the group); or else, intellectual material can be utilized within the T-group as part of the group design. In terms of the intellectual content of T-groups, the situation generates most dimensions of small group behavior with which academic social psychologists concern themselves: influence, conformity, leadership, decision-making, power, communication networks, roles, and deviance. The T-group is, after all, a social situation and will have elements of all social situations. As a basis of experience by which students can learn about formal social psychology, it is better than most other social situations because of the high degree of involvement on the part of participants. Because members get involved in the group and because the group is concerned with examining itself, members become very aware of what happened in the group and can easily think of it in the same terms that social psychologists think of social behavior. If lectures or role playing exercise are used in conjunction with the T-group, there is intellectual learning as well as emotional learning.

A number of years ago, when I was running T-groups at Enfield College of Technology in London, I did an experiment. It actually was not a planned experiment, but it turned out in retrospect to have been one. At the time, I was running six weekly groups. After about five weeks of meetings, I decided to give each group a lecture on group process and decision-making, mostly based on the work of *Bales* and his students (2). After another five meetings, I then gave each group a lecture on emotionality in groups and the expression of interpersonal needs, revolving around the work of *Bion* (5) and *Schutz* (29). The effect of these two lectures was limited. It seemed to have had some impact on the subsequent meetings, but at the end of the T-group meetings, the members could not remember much of either sets of theories.

The next year, I also had six weekly T-groups. But this time, I waited until all the T-group meetings had finished before introducing any theoretical material. I then gave on two successive weeks the same lectures that I had given the year before. This time, the effect was far more dramatic. The members of the groups understood the material far better than the previous year's members and they remembered the material for at least a year, when I discussed it with them again. The conclusion I drew from this was that the T-group had been useful in providing an experience which could help the learning of group theories, but that the group had to be finished in order to have this effect. I am not sure why this occurs in this way — perhaps because of some kind of closure in the students or because of a better perspective on the experience — but it seemed to be a real effect. I have not systematically tested what type of material is learned best after a T-group, but I would guess that it would be material which is related to what happened in the group itself.

T-groups can be a very viable experience for the learning of social psychological theory and they can also generate insights into groups for which social psychological theory is inadequate. In the last ten years, because of the growth of T-groups in American and British universities, there have developed a number of social psychological theories that have utilized T-group-type material (11, 30).

Role Playing as a Teaching Method

The use of active participation and emotional expression for the learning of intellectual experience extends beyond T-groups, however. Perhaps the oldest use of participation as a teaching method is that of role playing, which goes back to the 1920s (22). Role playing can be used to study all kinds of situations from issues concerning unique individuals to broader issues concerning an entire community. *Moreno,* probably the leading innovator in this area, used to distinguish between psychodrama (21), which examines individual feelings and assumptions, and sociodrama (20), which looks at relationships between people. Though the distinction is not a clear-cut one, as any social situation has both aspects, the wide range of phenomena encompassed by this technique can be seen. One could, presumably, design a role playing around any theoretical issue, act it out and then discuss it. The role playing and the discussion which follows creates a language around which theoretical ideas can be explored. The types of roles that can be examined vary from very unstructured roles, where the actor provides his own interpretation of the situation, thereby allowing the discussion to focus on how he interpreted it, to very structured situations where all actors more or less act in the same way. In this latter case, students learn that certain roles have restraints and obligations within them and come to an understanding of the limitations of these roles (e.g., policemen in a riot, traffic wardens, political crises situations).

Any theoretical material in social psychology can be looked at by role playing exercises. There are no rules about how to do it. It requires a bit of thought, a bit of imagination, some luck, and the ability to remember from one trial to another what went wrong the last time. To give a few examples in order to illustrate the range of possibilities for role playing, here is a list of a number of uses to which I have put role playing:

(1) To illustrate group decision-making: Have five members discuss a problem for 20 min and come to a decision. Other members sit around and act as observers. This is a very simple but effective way of introducing an emphasis on group process to students. If you tell the observers, for example, 'pay attention

to behaviors that help the group come to a decision and behaviors that inhibit the group from coming to a decision', then they will concentrate on watching how the group is going about their decision-making, and not just on what they are saying.

(2) To illustrate group conflict in decision-making: Take the same situation, but build in external obligations. 'You must defend this position, because your organization believes in ... Under no conditions are you to agree to ...' In this case, the participants' freedom to act in the situation is limited by the obligations. Conflict is an almost inevitable result with a decision being far more difficult to reach. This exercise is very useful for developing a discussion on the limits to freedom of action, the existence of conflict in social life, and the way in which organizations can perpetuate positions through their actors, even though the actors may disagree with the position.

(3) To illustrate the effect of hidden feelings on group process: Set up a committee of seven to discuss an 'important' issue (e.g., money to be spent). Two members are to be 10 min late. Explain that the exercise is to examine the effects of late members on group process. When the two late-members have gone out of the room, explain to the others that: 'Whoever sits in this seat is to be the favored member. And whoever sits in that seat is to be totally ignored.' The group then acts out the situation, and with the observers at the end, they discuss the effect of acceptance and rejection on the late-comers' behavior (after informing the two members of the deception, of course). Typically, rejected members tend to either withdraw from the situation and become bored or else they get angry and try to fight their way into the situation. The favored member becomes interested in the situation. This is a good example for illustrating how individual feelings are very often responses to assumptions made by other people.

(4) To explore male-female stereotypes: Have members act out their stereotypes of men and women. For example, have one member be the 'male' and the other member the 'female'. The male then telephones the female in order to ask her out for a cinema. This can be done sitting next to each other and the actors pretend to telephone each other. If sex roles are actually reversed (i.e. men play women and vice versa) substantial insight can be achieved into the stereotyped roles. Another variation is to have a male and a female apply for the same job. Even though the 'interviewer' may be trying to act neutrally to both, the implicit sex stereotypes come out.

(5) To illustrate teacher-student roles: Have one member play a 'teacher' and another a 'student' who is complaining about an exam grade. Even though the student playing the teacher may never have been a teacher before, he nevertheless acts like one. This is a good example for discussing how people learn social roles and how they often learn the reciprocal of the role, as well as the role itself.

(6) Role playings can be created around fantasy and the effect is often very

liberating. Here is one that I did once. To one student in a class, I handed an imaginary ball of string. 'Here, hold this end of this string.' I then unravelled the 'string' to still another student. 'Here, you take the string and tie things up.' After a few minutes of hesitation, the room became criss-crossed with imaginary lines of string that people were stepping over or crawling under. Because of the projective nature of the exercise, a number of issues will come up in discussion: how people can accept a fictitious definition of a situation, how group behavior revolves around a sense of consensus rather than necessarily something tangible, how people are able to show emotional identification with things, why people feel happy and liberated in the situation (which they usually do), and what is the nature of play and fun.

(7) To illustrate a basic experience of dependency: A colleague of mine, *Sheila Rossan,* has two students feed each other salad and asks the participants to act like 'parent' and 'child'. She televises the occasion and then plays it back in order to provide another dimension to the discussion. The situation is excellent for discussing feelings of parent–child relationships, what it feels like to be dependent, how trust or mistrust grows out of the situation as it develops (some 'parents' create trust in their 'child', while others create mistrust), and what it feels like to be publicly visible in a dependent position (i.e. the TV).

This list should be sufficient to illustrate the wide diversity of role playing situations that can be created. Each role playing situation creates a strong emotional identification by the students with the role; from this, a very elaborate discussion usually results. After students have become less involved in the role, various theoretical ideas can be introduced for which the students can rely on their experience in the role play. The learning that will occur is more real to the students and is integrated much more efficiently than more passive methods of learning, an effect demonstrated by a number of researchers (4, 17).

Gaming and Simulation as Methods of Teaching

Two other participation methods of learning – gaming and simulation – will be discussed together as they are both extensions of role playing techniques. The idea of play and games have been around human beings probably as long as there have been human societies. Virtually every child in any society participates in play and learns about the world and about expectations through the effect of play and games.

However, as a specific teaching method for older students, the use of these methods has not been developed very elaborately until quite recently. In the last ten years, there has emerged a new awareness of the possibilities of using social participation as a means of looking at complex and elaborate situations. Social scientists of many shades have become involved in the use of games and simulations in order to construct models of social reality. These techniques have varied from theoretical expositions of games and strategies (18) to simple experiments involving people making strategies in groups (24), to very complicated simulations of complex problems in international relations (13, 28). In all these studies, role playing is the basic technique as individuals are required to participate actively according to differents schemas. The situations differ, however, in whether they are a game or a simulation.

In a *game,* the individuals follow a set of rules which govern the situation. In this case, the individuals play themselves and they follow the rules, adopting various strategies if required. A formal solution is often sought, but is not necessary. The learning in these cases, for both the experimenters and the participants, is about what is possible in the situation. The game produces a result which is either governed by the rules, or by individual strategies, or by most probably an interaction between the two. The most obvious examples are the everyday games that people are familiar with: football, golf, tennis, etc. In all these cases, there are limits imposed by the rules, which tell the individuals how to play, when to play, what to do and what not to do, how to interpret conflict, and so forth. Individual strategies are seen by the differences between players or between the same player at different times. In terms of the concept of a game, it is immaterial whether or not the individuals are aware of their strategies; it is merely necessary that they act according to the rules and that violations of the rules are not permitted. In terms of social research, games such as 'prisoner's dilemma' (25) have been studied almost to an excess, while other examples are by *Deutsch and Krauss* (8) and *Hausner et al.* (14). Aside from research games, commercial games have been around for a long time now (e.g., 'monopoly', 'diplomacy'); these can be seen as both a learning experience or a toy, depending on your orientation. Gaming, after all, is a way of learning for adults, much as toys and simpler games are means of learning for children.

In a *simulation,* individuals attempt to simulate a real-life situation by trying to act in a way to make that real situation emerge. In this case, individuals usually act out roles, rather than play themselves. In complex situations, there are often rules and game elements along with the role playing. A very complex simulation involves several different levels of interaction. To give some examples, the notorious 'war games' of the Rand Corporation and the Pentagon are the most famous. Research uses of simulations have involved a general international relations situation (13), a Middle East simulation[2], and a student-university confrontation[3]. The particular roles, rules, and venue will vary from situation to situation.

To illustrate, recently at Brunel University, a class of mine designed a North-

2 This was run by the Institute of Strategic Studies in London, in 1966.
3 *Ed Sampson* and I developed a student-administration simulation in 1971.

ern Ireland simulation which ran for five hours one day. Players were given roles and then placed in teams in different rooms. Different roles were given different rules and some players had more power and flexibility than other players (e.g., the Prime Minister of the UK compared to a catholic in the Northern Ireland catholic community team). Rules about communication were established in which face-to-face communication, telephone contact, mass media communications, contacts through intermediaries, and 'travel' were allowed depending on the role involved and the situation. Within the simulation, two games were also included: an economic game and a military game. The players, therefore, had not only to act out the political simulation, but they had to play the two games according to the rules. In this way, we created a fairly complex situation which involved numerous strategies and possibilities. The simulation was highly involving for the participants and the discussion which followed provided an additional learning experience as the situation was critically evaluated. Points in the simulation which were not realistic compared to the real situation were discussed and this provided more material for thought.

A simulation, therefore, allows individuals to become involved in a role, to experience some of the feelings associated with the role, and to become sensitive to many of the constraints and limits imposed on by a role. These feelings are essential to understanding any role and allow individuals to come to a better awareness of the roles in the real world. While the use of simulation has been criticized methodologically as a means for studying real-life situations and producing knowledge (10), as a means for teaching students about outside reality, it is extremely useful. First, simulations can allow individuals to learn about situations to which they do not have access. We found after our Northern Ireland simulation that a number of students suddenly became aware of what was happening in Northern Ireland. Whereas previously, though they had known intellectually about what was happening, the situation had no emotional meaning for them and, consequently, they were uninvolved. After the simulation, these individuals suddenly realized a number of things that the real participants must be feeling and, consequently, they became more involved in reading the newspapers each day. The simulation provided them an emotionality on which to hang their intellectual ideas.

Second, simulations are useful as a means of generating hypotheses and predictions about certain situations. While one can do this merely by reading and discussing the situation, by setting up a complex role play and having individuals act out the various roles, often unintended possibilities open up from the actual behavior of the participants. The simulation is a way of elaborating on theoretical ideas. Before doing an expensive study on a social situation, it is more efficient to first test out a researcher's ideas by having individuals act out various roles in the situation. By watching how participants behave, a student or a researcher can see to what extent his ideas are plausible. If they prove so, he can then go out and do the actual research. In this way, the use of simulation is comparable to the use of analogues that engineers and designers build first for testing. Rather than commit an entire production system to make something, it is much cheaper to first build a small model which can be tested on a number of points.

Third, simulations are a far more ethical method of teaching students than other methods which require deception and misrepresentation. In the last few years, there have been intense criticisms leveled against the methods sometimes used in social and psychological research (7, 15, 26). There have been complaints made against social scientists and psychologists that they do not adequately consider their subjects. Subjects have been deceived, tricked, made anxious, and manipulated, all in the name of science. In a number of known cases, actual psychological damage has been inflicted on subjects for participating in a particular research, whether it was a psychological experiment or a field study. The situation became so bad, in fact, that the Congress of the United States opened hearings on the misuse of psychological testing in industry, the civil service, and in education (1). Anthropologists have also become concerned about the ethics of their profession (6). The particular criticisms directed against social psychologists is that in order to study social behavior, many use experiments in which subjects are deceived in order to produce the 'desired experimental effect'. While most social psychologists who use deception will explain the purpose of the experiment to the subject after the experiment is finished, the long-term consequences of the deception have not been properly considered. Aside from the fact that the results extracted from experiments have been accused of being invalid in any case (23, 27), the use of deception creates dangerous possibilities that in many cases do not warrant the research.

With simulation, many of these problems are eliminated. All the participants are aware of what is happening in the situation and all gain from the situation as they are all experimenters. Further, all take part in the discussion and help criticize the experiment in a way that a usual subject in an experiment is never allowed to do. Further, there have been several studies where the use of simulation was compared to the use of deception and the results were not unfavorable (12, 32). Simulations are a useful method for teaching students and for exploring social research.

But it is at this point that the use of group techniques merges with other techniques that are used for studying people and various aspects of society. For a social scientist who is using simulation is also trying to understand the way people in society behave, the way in which people with their unique personalities interact with the social structure. And anyone studying in this area is well aware that an individual's behavior is not only determined by his own unique self but that his thoughts, actions, and feelings are also affected by the economic, political, and social world around him. The person is not totally free and he must learn to accommodate to other people around him and to the structures that organize these people. Reality is, really, this way, and if group training is to be of any use in society, it must be reconciled with the constraints of that outside world.

Conclusion

T-groups, role playing, games and simulations are all techniques that are useful in examining people within social contexts. Each of these techniques for teaching have a different emphasis, but they all have a number of elements in common. First, they all depend on active participation. The student must participate in order to learn, rather than sit back as in the more traditional methods of teaching. In this way, these techniques represent a growing trend in universities and colleges to introduce more active methods of learning for students, to accompany the more traditional methods (lectures, seminars, reading). Few people have advocated the outright rejection of the 'old' methods, but many do feel that they may not be the most appropriate ways of encouraging independence and stimulating creativity. Participation methods, on the other hand, require that the student discover things for himself.

Second, these methods all depend on empathy as a necessary ingredient in the learning process. In the more traditional methods of learning, emotional identity is not necessary in order to learn things; one just sits back and takes it in, on an intellectual level. But this way of learning is in some ways false. Especially with social science, people's behavior relies on feelings and understandings. To deny a student access to those feelings and understandings is to virtually cut him off from what is really happening. One cannot, as a social or psychological observer, sit back and view the world objectively; people do not behave objectively, but in terms of their perceptions and the assumptions they make. Even where there is formal structure in the real world, this structure is really only a set of assumptions that people have made; it may be difficult to change those assumptions, but they still exist only because of consensus. 'Man made society and man can change society' is an old cliché, but it asserts the necessity of social meanings and feelings. T-groups, role playings, simulations require a participant to identify with what is happening and to become aware within himself of his feelings in the situation, and it is this emotional identification which allows him to understand why people do what they do.

Third, these methods all require participation between people. Interaction with other individuals is a necessary component in active learning. Helping, cooperating with, and even fighting with others is necessary in order to make the situation develop and to allow the individual to learn. In the more traditional methods of teaching, interaction between individuals is often at a minimum. Reading requires no other people in the situation. Lectures require only one lecturer who talks, with an almost nonexistent interaction between the audience.

In seminars, there is more interaction, but in most cases where one person reads out a paper, interaction here is relatively minimal. There is something very important which is missing in the usual educational methods of teaching and this is the participation between students. If the subject matter is so exact and so predetermined as to be fundamental for learning, then there are grounds for using lectures and one-way teaching methods. But in psychology and social science, the amount of material that has to be taught this way is quite small. Even with well-established theories, students often have to rediscover the elements for themselves and cannot depend on the word of an expert. Participation methods, therefore, allow students to develop their resources by interacting with other students, as well as with a teacher, and the product of what they create is dependent on that interaction. Learning, then, becomes a process which is changing and developing rather than a fixed quantity of information churned out from some book or computer. Further, students feel they have participated in something active and creative and come out with a sense of having achieved something.

Higher education is undergoing a critical period right now. Assumptions about teaching and about knowledge are being questioned and analyzed in the light of what that knowledge does in society and for whom it is. There is an increasing demand for an active process of education supplementing a more standard form of education, and there are strong movements to bring the society into the institute, rather than to keep it separate. Participation methods of learning are one small development towards a more relevant and active educational experience; and while they certainly do not constitute answers to all problems, they, nevertheless, represent a step forward. And it is to this direction that I look forward in the near future.

References

1 American Psychologist: About special privilege and special responsibility. Amer. Psychol. *20:* 857–993 (1965).
2 *Bales, R.F.:* Adaptive and integrative changes as sources of strain in social systems; in *Hare, Borgatta and Bales* Small groups, pp. 127–131 (Knopf, New York 1962).
3 *Beckett, S.:* Waiting for Godot. Tragicomedy in two acts (Grove Press, New York 1954).
4 *Bennett, E.B.:* Discussion, decision, commitment, and consensus in 'group decision'. Human Relat. *8:* 251–273 (1955).
5 *Bion, W.R.:* Experiences in groups (Basic Books, New York 1959).
6 Current Anthropology: Special issue on responsibility in anthropology. Curr. Anthrop. (May 1968).
7 Daedalus: Issue on ethical aspects of experimentation with human subjects. Daedalus *98* (1969).
8 *Deutsch, M. and Krauss, R.M.:* Studies of interpersonal bargaining. J. Conflict Resol. *6:* 52–76 (1962).

9   Erikson, E.H.: The problem of ego identity. J. amer. psychoanal. Ass. 4: 56–121
    (1956).
10 Freedman, J.L.: Role playing: psychology by consensus. J. pers. soc. Psychol. 13:
    107–114 (1969).
11 Garfinkel, H.: Studies in ethnomethodology (Prentice-Hall, Englewood Cliffs 1967).
12 Greenberg, M.S.: Role playing: an alternative to deception? J. pers. soc. Psychol. 7:
    152–157 (1967).
13 Guetzkow, H.: A use of simulation in the study of international relations. Behav. Sci.
    4: 183–191 (1959).
14 Hausner, M.; Nash, J.F.; Shapley, L.S., and Shubik, M.: 'So long sucker', a four-person
    game; in Shubik Game theory and related approaches to social behavior, pp. 359–361
    (Wiley, New York 1964).
15 Kelman, H.C.: A time to speak: on human values and social research (Jossey-Bass, San
    Francisco 1968).
16 Levine, N.: Emotional factors in group development. Human Relat. 24: 65–89 (1971).
17 Lewin, K.: Group decision and social change; in Maccoby, Newcomb and Hartley
    Readings in social psychology; 3rd ed., pp. 197–211 (Holt, Rinehart & Winston, New
    York 1958).
18 Luce, R.D. and Raiffa, H.: Games and decisions (Wiley, New York 1957).
19 Mills, T.M.: Group transformation: an analysis of a learning group (Prentice-Hall,
    Englewood Cliffs 1964).
20 Moreno, J.L.: Sociodrama: a method for the analysis of social conflicts (Beacon House,
    Beacon 1944).
21 Moreno, J.L.: Psychodrama, vol. 1 (Beacon House, Beacon 1946).
22 Moreno, J.L.: The theatre of spontaneity (Beacon House, Beacon 1947).
23 Orne, M.T.: On the social psychology of the psychological experiment: with particular
    reference to demand characteristics and their implications. Amer. Psychol. 17: 776–
    783 (1962).
24 Rapoport, A. and Orwant, C.: Experimental games: a review. Behav. Sci. 7: No. 1
    (1962).
25 Rapoport, A. and Chammah, A.: Prisoner's dilemma: a study in conflict and coopera-
    tion (University of Michigan Press, Ann Arbor 1965).
26 Rapoport, R.N.: Three dilemmas in action research. Human Relat. 23: 499–513
    (1970).
27 Rosenthal, R.: The effect of the experimenter on the results of psychological research;
    in Maher Progress in experimental personality research, vol. 1 (Academic Press, New
    York 1964).
28 Schelling, T.C.: Experimental games and bargaining theory. World Politics 14: 47–68
    (1961).
29 Schutz, W.C.: FIRO: a three-dimensional theory of interpersonal behavior (Holt, Rine-
    hart & Winston, New York 1958).
30 Slater, P.E.: Microcosm: structural, psychological and religious evolution in groups
    (Wiley, New York 1966).
31 Whittaker, D.S. and Lieberman, M.A.: Psychotherapy through the group process
    (Atherton Press, New York 1964).
32 Willis, R.H. and Willis, Y.A.: Role playing versus deception: an experimental compari-
    son. J. pers. soc. Psychol. 16: 472–477 (1970).

Author's address: Dr. Ned Levine, Department of Psychology, Brunel University,
Uxbridge, Middlesex (England)

Interpers. Develop. *3:* 68–79 (1972)

The Development of Group Training in a Civil Service Ministry

D.J. Page

Sheppard, Moscow and Associates, Management Consultants, London

Early Origins

In 1965, the newly formed (UK) Ministry of Technology started a programme of 5-day junior management courses for higher executive officers and equivalent. For the most part, these courses consisted of theory and application sessions on subjects such as interviewing, communication, performance appraisal, principles of management and organisation, together with obligatory set-piece lectures on security and welfare, which all Civil Service Courses customarily contained. However, a half-day slot entitled 'Decision-Making Skills' was offered to the North Western Polytechnic of London, whose experiential learning methods had impressed the ministry trainers at a public seminar earlier in the year. Initially, these half-day sessions were handled in a fairly structured way, with half the group performing a task whilst the other half observed the process. As the series of six courses progressed, these half-day sessions became more and more successful, until it was possible to take a few more risks. The result was that they became 'mini-T-groups', provoking considerable interest within a newly created and highly innovative training team in the new ministry. By mid-1966, sessions on group dynamics had been formally introduced into junior and middle management courses throughout the ministry. A few months later, this relatively small Ministry of Technology was involved in a merger with the much larger Ministry of Aviation, and the training team which had initiated the use of group dynamics was taken over by the Ministry of Aviation's internal training department. The interest provoked by the pilot series of courses was such that the head of the combined department initiated new talks with the North Western Polytechnic, consequent upon which a 3-day group dynamics module was built into both the middle management and senior management courses, which ran for the following 2 years at the rate of 15 or more courses per year. *Colin Sheppard,* who pioneered this work on behalf of the North Western Polytechnic, was accompanied on each occasion by various members of the internal training department of the ministry and gradually, by means of this informal co-trainer role, a body of experiential skills and awareness was built up within the department. Meanwhile, the demand for the courses was increasing and an awareness of the potential of experiential group learning began to permeate other areas of training. In consequence of this, and following the appointment of a new head of internal training towards the end of 1968, it was decided to initiate a formal trainer development programme to increase the body of group skills and conceptual awareness within the ministry's training branch as a whole. This event was designed and undertaken by a firm of management consultants — Sheppard, Moscow and Associates — which contained many of the same team of trainers who had worked for the North Western Polytechnic on the earlier courses, prior to becoming a private enterprise.

The Trainer Development Programme – Preliminary Considerations

The particular design chosen for the trainer development programme originated from the fact that there was a wide spectrum of skill, experience and awareness of group dynamics methods across the internal training department. At one extreme was a small section whose whole existence and mode of daily operation centred round a value system of 'non-directedness' and who were consequently experiencing problems of relating to the Civil Service hierarchy and to the other parts of the department who were not immersed in the ideology to anything like the same extent. On the other flank were a group of very experienced lecturers whose main activity centred around the running of induction and other courses in Civil Service Organisation using a fairly traditional structured mould. To them, group dynamics was seen variously as an alien cult, and as the passport to promotion and advancement within the training function.

In between these extremes, there were a number of other trainers, more or less experienced in group dynamics, whose job requirements involved them in working on both structured and unstructured training. To cope with this range of skills and needs, the trainer team produced a 3-phase plan, with intermediate arrangements for securing individual continuity of experience.

Phase 1 was a series of 8 seminars, each of 2 h duration, backed by guided reading on a number of theoretical topics. These were held in the evenings because of the difficulty of getting the trainer group together in the daytime, and they provided the basic groundwork on to which the later experiential training was grafted. During this phase of the programme, participants were also required (where this had not previously been achieved) to undertake at least one T-group as a participant and at least one as an 'apprentice' to a more experienced T-group trainer.

The central phase of the programme, a non-residential course lasting 2 weeks, was almost entirely practical and experiential, designed to give participants a shared experience of a T-group, aided by some intra- and inter-group exercises and an opportunity to practise the craft of T-group trainer under skilled supervision. At the end of this course, the 3 consultant trainers jointly made and shared with the individual a confidential assessment of that individual's suitability as a T-group trainer. To enrich the processes and give greater variety to the interactions, a third dimension was added to the participant membership at this stage by bringing in 4 or 5 experienced trainers (including the author) from outside the ministry, who were also ready for an advanced development programme.

Activities during the Central Phase of the Trainer Development Programme

The time-table for this central phase of the development programme is shown in table I. The three faculty members *(Colin Sheppard, David Moscow and Mel Berger)* had previously decided the composition of the two T-groups with 9 members and one trainer in each. The initial division was made into an 'advanced' group, consisting of those participants who already had experience of working as T-group trainers, either inside or outside the ministry or both, and an 'elementary' group, whose members' previous experience of group dynamics was at participant level only. This differentiation, in itself, made an important contribution to the climate of both the T-group sessions and the inter-group exercises in the second week. In general, the advanced group concerned itself with a number of inter-personal rivalries, the members seeking to impress one another with their diagnostic and interpretative skills, whilst settling a number of old scores concerned with the power structure within the ministry training branch. Meanwhile, the other group became highly counter-dependent with many members expressing strong objections to the whole cult of group dynamics! However, this gap in sophistication between the two groups was partially bridged, and their learning to some extent shared, by reserving one session daily for the first 3 days in which mixed 'project groups' could meet to compare progress in the two groups. These consisted of subgroups of 4 or 5 of mixed representation, whose job it was to look at and share the issues, the developing norms, the unmet needs and members' own intentions in their respective groups. The catalytic effect of these daily sessions (preceded by 10 min private 'diary time') was undeniable, and compensated to some degree for the limitations of a non-residential course.

On the fourth day of the first week, the character of the activity changed and a review was made, using a structure of 'helping trios' from each group, of the personal style of each member. This was followed, later on the same day, by a more systematic comparison of the results achieved in the two groups. This led

Table 1. Time-table for the 2-week course (phase 2 of the trainer development programme)

	Monday	Tuesday	Wednesday	Thursday	Friday
Week 1					
9.15–10.45	orientation; T-groups	T-groups	T-groups	analysis groups (group devt. and trainer skills)	trainer role practice
11.00–12.45	T-groups	non-verbal techniques	T-groups	analysis groups, continued	trainer role practice
1.45–3.00	project groups	T-groups	project groups	project groups (comparing analyses)	trainer role practice
3.15–5.30	T-groups	project groups	T-groups	analysis groups, continued	trainer role practice
Evening	free discussion	tape listening	tape listening (optional)		
Week 2					
9.15–10.45	re-orientation; interactive decision-making	inter-group implementation exercise	large group	inter-group problem diagnosis	theory on lab. design and trainer styles
11.00–12.45	inter-group perceptions	analysis and theory of inter-group	assessment and collation of unmet needs	inter-group problem solving	individual counselling and evaluation
1.45–3.00	inter-group planning exercise	inter-group	implementation of unmet needs	large group, analysis and theory	individual counselling and evaluation
3.15–5.30	inter-group planning exercise	inter-group exercise and implementation	implementation of unmet needs	individual preparation	course review

naturally to the following day's activity in which the project group structure was used to represent a mini-T-group with a visiting 'trainer' from another project group. This activity, lasting for 1 h followed by 15 min feedback, was repeated three times during the day, thus providing each member of the course with the opportunity of taking the trainer role in a group with which he was relatively unfamiliar.

Week 2 began with an interactive decision-making exercise, familiarly known as 'the prisoner's dilemma', which provided a preliminary insight into phenomena of competitiveness and cooperation between interdependent groups. This was followed by the first major inter-group exercise, involving the advanced, the elementary and the staff groups, in separate rooms, comparing perceptions of themselves and of the other two groups via the exchange of observers, delegates and plenipotentiaries. An interesting phenomenon was the reversal of competence which apparently took place during this exercise between the so-called advanced group (who had started 'fat and happy' but whose internal divisions were soon revealed by the others), and the so-called elementary group, whose relatively skilful outgoing activity in the face of a common enemy soon cured their 'lean and hungry' look from the previous week. After sharing these perceptions in a plenary session, the three groups then separated again to plan an activity designed to make their perceptions of one another more accurate. By the end of this exercise, the structure had become much more fluid and relationships between the two groups were no longer as strained as they had been. Wednesday of the second week was designed to enable activities to be scheduled which would satisfy members' residual unmet needs. After a period of individual 'think time', lists were produced by each member and pinned to their person, so that by a process of milling around the room a quick tally could be made of common interest areas leading to the formation of *ad hoc* groupings for implementation of the revealed needs.

For the final inter-group exercise on the Thursday, two new groups were formed, each containing 50 % of the membership of the original two groups, except for two assigned observers who played no part in the proceedings but merely collected data for the information bank. The task of these new groups, using the previously established machinery for exchanging representatives, was to agree jointly on a problem within the context of the course objectives, which both groups saw as being worth solving. Finally, the experience of the previous 4 days of inter-group working was summated and viewed against background theory and research findings, in a large group session. As an overnight activity, members were then asked to give careful consideration to a number of questions affecting their attitude towards their personal future as group dynamics trainers, in preparation for individual counselling on the following day. For those who decided that they wished to pursue this type of work, a report on the counselling session and on the staff team's recommendations, was forwarded confidentially to the head of internal training for the ministry.

Intermediate Assignments outside the Ministry

Between the completion of phase 2 of the trainer development programme and the final phase 6 months later, selected individuals were given a number of external training assignments with commercial and industrial firms, working as co-trainers with more experienced full-time consultants and associates from the staff of Sheppard, Moscow and Associates, to broaden their experience in other cultures. These external client contacts included assignments in the motor industry, the chemical industry and the hotel and catering trades, involving both structured and unstructured laboratory and workshop designs. Meanwhile, the ministry's own courses continued to gather momentum, developing a greater range of creativity and effectiveness via the combination of internal and external trainers who had by this time developed more trust and insight into one another's styles and aspirations.

The Final Phase – A Look at Organisation Development Concepts

The final phase of the development programme was a 5-day residential workshop, held at a hotel in Weybridge, England, during April, 1970. By this time, a number of former participants (mainly from the 'elementary' group in phase 2) had been eliminated from the trainer development population by personal choice, by internal transfer or by adverse recommendation, so that the participants of the third phase numbered only 12.

The objectives of this third phase centred round the conversion and adaptation of trainer skills and awareness into the broader concepts of organisation development, i.e. to give the trainers a chance to reconsider their role as possible change agents within the ministry. To this end, a series of visiting consultants *(Fred van Ravenswaaij, Eve Godfrey, David Moscow and Peter B. Smith)* each spent about a day with the participant group, helping members to understand the concepts, the difficulties and the implications for themselves and the ministry of such a change of role. The subject areas touched upon during each of these sessions are shown on table II. It is difficult to convey adequately the flavour of the group's activities during this workshop. One recurring issue, however, was the way in which the groups used the visiting consultants – were they to be regarded as experts who had a tale to tell, or should they rather be allowed to model the client-centred (organisation development) consultant in the way they brought out the inherent resources of the group? Each of the visitors illustrated by his or her behaviour their competence and willingness to perform in either role, whilst the participants demonstrated the full range of behaviour from dependency to counter-dependency towards the visitors, depending (it would seem) on their individual assessment of their own expertise as change agents!

Table II. One-week residential workshop (phase 3 of the trainer development programme; emergent design, with the following visitors and topic areas)

	Times	Visitor	Topics
Monday	2.15–6.15 8.15–9.30	*Fred Van Ravenswaaij*	architecture and strategy for total change programmes; the consultant's role
Tuesday	9.15–6.15 8.15–9.30	*Fred Van Ravenswaaij*	force field analysis as diagnostic tool, applied to ministry situation; diagnosis of conversion needs from trainer to change agent, at organisational and individual level
Wednesday	9.15–6.15 8.15–9.30	*Eve Godfrey*	the internal and external change agent; frameworks for OD strategies and the setting of change goals; diagnostic tools application to case study and to ministry situation
Thursday	9.15–6.15 8.15–9.30	*David Moscow*	similarities and differences of trainer V change agent; conversion programmes; learning models for individuals and organisations; constructive dissonance; pre- and post-laboratory work; stranger, cousin and family training groups
Friday	9.15–12.15	*Peter Smith*	effect of trainer style and participant mix variations on the achievement of specific learning goals; research designs and interim findings

Table III. Management of human resources (residential 2-week course programme)

	9.15–10.45	Coffee	11.15–12.45	Lunch	2.15–3.45	Tea	4.15–5.15	Dinner	8.15–9.45
Sunday								introduction	small group activities
Monday	small group activities								staff reporting exercise
Tuesday	small group activities								
Wednesday	small group activities						selection interviewing, briefing and preparation		free period
Thursday	staff development						appraisal interviewing		
Friday	staff reporting								free
Monday	small group activities				selection interviewing				
Tuesday	inter-group activities								
Wednesday	small group activities		organisational exercise						management by objectives
Thursday	management by objectives								free period
Friday	welfare		final discussion		free				

Issues like this one, coupled with a number of 'back-home' rivalries, produced a number of unscheduled T-groups, both within and outside the official working sessions. As a result, a greater amount of trust developed within the group of ministry trainers, and also between them and the external visiting members of the group, who were about equal in number on this occasion.

The Consequences of Ministry Reorganisations

It is unfortunate, perhaps, that before the lessons of this final week could be put into practice, a major change took place in the structure of the ministry and in the position of the education and training branch in relation to its client population, following the change of government in Britain. This factor, followed by two further major external upheavals in the ensuing two years, has virtually killed for the time being, any possible initiatives that the internal training team might have taken as change agents beyond the realm of training courses.

In these reduced circumstances, therefore, the results of the trainer development programme can be measured only in terms of improved training technology (including both the design and handling), and the evaluation of subsequent courses.

The Management of Human Resources

The major outcome, in terms of new training activities, has been a completely new, and very successful 2-week residential course entitled 'The Management of Human Resources', which was designed collectively by the group of ministry trainers who had been through the development programme. This multi-level course has replaced the former 'middle management' and 'senior management' 1-week courses with their segregated populations, and has brought in the added sophistication of inter-group and organisational simulations which had been part of the learning during the second phase of the trainer development programme.

The staffing of this activity has once again been a combination of internal trainers and visiting consultants (usually in the ratio of 3:1, but sometimes 2:2, depending on the current loading of other types of work upon the ministry team). The published programme, illustrated in table III, has remained unchanged for the past 2.5 years, and courses of 24 participants have been held at the rate of 6 or 7 a year during that period, which means that between 300 and 400 alumni are now distributed in various parts of the Civil Service following the disbandment and regrouping of the Ministry of Technology. Throughout its life, this course has been carefully monitored by means of a detailed post-course assessment form, and the very positive response of participants has helped it to survive despite a number of adverse moves by pressure groups who are anxious to put an end to all forms of group dynamics training (and to this course in particular) on the grounds that it is undermining the accepted Civil Service culture! In fact, these post-course assessments have consistently met the 80-percent yardstick, which the trainers regard as the measure of satisfactory performance. This means that, of the 5 possible overall satisfaction rating categories provided on the form, 80 % or more of respondents have consistently rated it in the top 2 categories.

Although the published programme has remained unchanged, the actual innovations and variations within this framework have been legion — each different combination of internal and external trainers having burnt a great deal of midnight oil to produce diagnoses and appropriately tailor-made activities to suit the particular groups of participants and emergent situations that have arisen. There is nothing stereotyped about these courses at the Beach Hotel, Littlehampton, and the training rooms there contain many 'ghosts' of new ideas which went particularly well, or particularly badly! Any attempt on the author's part, therefore, to describe a 'typical' sequence of activities on these courses would do scant justice to the wealth of creativity which these late night planning sessions have produced. However, it is usual to start with some kind of 'mini-lab' activity on the first Sunday evening, to give the participants a chance to unfreeze a little, to examine the resources available, and to make decisions (somewhat superficially, it usually transpires) affecting the division into small groups, the allocation of groups to rooms, and frequently also the allocation of trainers to groups. This open decision-making, followed by a brief analysis of the decision-making process, has been found to have a useful catalytic effect on the subsequent small group sessions, by providing a shared experience not too far removed from the 'here-and-now'. Apart from one preparatory session on the Monday evening for a ministry-related staff reporting exercise, these basic T-group sessions usually continue uninterrupted until midday on Wednesday, when there is another preparatory session followed by a very welcome free evening. This usually has the effect of completing the basic ice-breaking between course members, and sometimes embraces the staff as well! Having avoided theory inputs up to this point in the course (usually, though not invariably), the following day's session on staff development includes some conceptual learning on the topic of motivation, sometimes by means of a 'mini-*Herzberg*) simulation, followed by a link-up with *Maslow*'s need hiearchy. The appraisal interviewing session later on the same day usually takes the form of counselling triads, rotating so that each member is 'appraised' by at least one other member on his performance on the course to date, with a third party observer who later appraises the appraiser. The week ends with a look at the ministry's staff reporting scheme or schemes, with the aid of a case study from which members can compare their wide range of ratings for the same set of facts, and thus gain insight into how subjective and biased it is possible to be when reporting on their subordinates.

After the week-end break, the T-groups re-form for two further sessions on the Monday morning, to try to regenerate some of the atmosphere of the previous week. The afternoon and evening then consist of a completely different activity, prepared the previous week, with simulated selection panels and candidates applying formally for fictitious jobs. This is designed to expose some of the hidden dynamics present in all such interviews and the skills necessary to overcome them. (It also has the spin-off of enriching the cross-group dynamics in readiness for the following day.) The inter-group exercise on the Tuesday is usually preceded by the most lengthy planning session of the week and usually exposes various tensions amongst the trainer team. All manner of different exercises have been tried at this stage, some based on a 'co-operation', some on a 'conflict' and some on a 'process-oriented' model. There is no one preferred design. The final 'small group activities' session on Wednesday morning usually provides an opportunity for the groups to metaphorically 'lick their wounds' from the inter-group activity, and to sort out any internal unfinished business. The organisational exercise which follows frequently takes the form of a competitive-tendering tower-building exercise, with a group of four elected 'managers' from one T-group supervising a group of eight 'artisans' from the other group, and vice versa. It is not unusual for industrial action to occur amongst the artisans as a reaction against their inept managers, and this provides the basis for a conceptual input later in the day on managerial styles. A brief practical exposure to the ministry's approach to management by objectives is then used to form a bridge between the course learning and the members' back-home job situations, and there is usually a social event of some kind to round off Thursday evening and the experiential part of the course. Friday's proceedings (accompanied frequently by headaches and dark glasses!) consist of a talk by a visiting ministry welfare officer, with its accompanying culture shock, and a final session to clear up the paperwork.

The Position in 1972

Following yet another organisational shuffle, the human resources course has now been transferred to the Ministry of Defence management centre. Ironically, all of the original participants of the trainer development programme have now been split off from the internal training branch which originally sponsored it, and the banner is being carried forward by two members of the original group, supported by a number of 'second-generation' trainers whom they themselves have trained. Life in the Civil Service being what it is, particularly in the current post-*Fulton*[1] atmosphere of de-specialisation, perhaps this is the most realistic way in which organisation development can be progressed at this stage, i.e. by the seeding of group trainers and course participants into other departments and ministries, until such time as a mandate is obtained for a more strategic approach.

Certainly with the benefits of hindsight, group dynamics in the Ministry of Technology and its successors has an enormous number of achievements to its credit that could hardly have been dreamt of back in those early days of 1965 when the first half-day sessions were organised for higher executive officers in the ministry.

1 The *Fulton* report is a British government document on the organisation of the Civil Service.

Author's address: *Denys J. Page,* Grove House, 54 Maidstone Road, *Rochester, Kent* (England)

Interpers. Develop. *3:* 80–99 (1972)

Group Training within an Organisation Development Project in an Industrial Company

Kenneth Harrison

Department of Management Sciences, University of Manchester Institute of Science and Technology, Manchester

The Background

Training is not Organisation Development

In organisation development (OD) theory, a great variety of change strategies are possible (2, 4). Many of these include 'normative re-educative' approaches (3) which, in turn, often use group training methods.

In practice, many organisations have experience of training, including management development, but are less familiar with the wider role of the organisational change agent or other action-centred strategies.

One consequence of the increasing interest in OD, combined with a need to cope with even the small changes necessary to establish the organisation development agency or strategy, has been a confusion between training and OD (both administratively and operationally). Managers, and even personnel managers, often know what the problems are in the organisation or department; they know where the bottle-necks are; who is not pulling his weight; and they have ideas as to what might be done about these problems. Instead of confronting the question of why this is so, the company mounts a training programme, instead of organisational change and development. Often the results include ritualistic, incestuous, over-elaborate, levy recovery oriented, irrelevant, training programmes which are the pride and joy of the training staff but have little reality in the client system.

This paper describes group work in the educational phases of a substantial OD project. The early stages of the project were very much in danger from the 'let's-train-not-change' approach discussed above. By combining the kind of training which has impact on participants with a high level of confrontation between internal change agents and the top management system, it was possible to develop from these early problems to a better understanding of the relationship between training and OD.

Thus, in our concern for the more detailed aspects of group training, it is important to keep in mind the dual frame of reference, that the group training was part of a larger OD project, and that, in turn, the OD project operated within the client organisation.

Outline of the Start-Up of the OD Project

A manufacturing division of a large industrial international company was faced with organisational problems which were not fully understood. Being a chemical process industry with high capital investment and elaborate technology, relatively little attention had been paid to the human resources aspect of the business.

Some data were available, including comparisons with similar operations elsewhere, which suggested that the main operating unit employing about 3,000 people was not efficient. Other data included feelings of low morale, high turnover of young graduates, low co-operation between departments, defensive attitudes among middle and senior managers, and growing dissatisfaction amongst supervisory staff.

First discussions were between senior management and the management development manager from the training department – in line with the lack of clarity as to the relationship between training and organisational change current in 1968–1969. These discussions led to external consultants (including the author) being called in to advise on training strategies. The company was familiar with the use of 'product consultants' but not with 'process consultants' (13). They consequently assumed that the consultants would sell them ready-made solutions to their problems.

An obvious starting point would have been to carry through a diagnostic phase (1) in which a better understanding of the role of the interventionists could have been developed by both the consultants and the managers concerned. This would also have to enable managers at all levels to identify the nature of their own problems prior to developing their own change plans in conjunction with others. These notions created high anxiety at senior management level. They were reluctant to share this activity with other staff and were unhappy about embarking on a project without more definite aims and procedures. They were unwilling and unable to examine their own problems and behaviour and generally felt that the fault lay with others – hence training was required!

This forms a diagnosis in itself. Top management were unable to develop any participation and problem-solving involvement with lower levels; low tolerance of ambiguity; low trust amongst senior managers; low willingness to examine own behaviour; and passing of responsibility for change onto others.

During these early discussions, relationships between external consultants, internal managers, and training staff were somewhat strained. It was as though the very presence of 'helpers' constituted an embarrassment or admission of inadequacy on the part of the company. Before the project had gone very far, the management development manager left the company and an element of scapegoating may have enabled the management to proceed more confidently. With the benefit of hindsight it is possible to see how the external consultants might have been more effective in their relationship with the company but, at the time, it appeared that a high level of confrontation would have been necessary to bring these various issues into open discussion and planning. Such a confrontation, with so anxious a client, could have led to a complete reaction against any realistic change strategy in favour of a complete training strategy. The kind of problems which led to the project were very influential in the start-up of the project itself.

A compromise approach was developed. This involved a project with educational phases aimed at increased awareness and adaptability, plus a change phase in which managers could initiate their own change plans. This approach admitted the preference which the company had towards training and used this as a 'lead-in' to organisational change. The hopeful assumption was that the educational phases would increase confidence and competence to start on change projects; the minimal result would be no less than the 'training-instead-of-change' strategy which had been a possibility.

This kind of design was operated as a pilot scheme on a small group of the top management. They took part in a programme which introduced or developed some concepts with which to examine organisational behaviour; some exercises which revealed some of their own problems and assumptions; and they took as their change project the decision concerning OD strategy in the unit.

Following this pilot exercise, top management made a decision to proceed with the strategy which had been evolved – with some reservations. The project was to be called 'The Development of Managerial Skills' and not OD – reflecting the basic diagnosis. Two full-time internal consultants were recruited to work with the external consultants initially in progressing the scheme. Top management even wished to locate these new resources within the training department, but this was successfully resisted, though they were established within the personnel function as a new department.

The project has operated for over two years and the responsibility for maintaining and developing it has naturally passed to the internal consultants – who, in turn, have established helpful relationships with other external consultants, whose skills were more relevant for the kind of work which is currently being undertaken. Over the last year, the company has experienced increasing business problems related to the excess of capacity over demand in this kind of product, cancellation of capital expansion projects, and the general recession common to many sectors of British industry at this time. These have led to a policy of 'business rationalisation' with 'voluntary severance', whereby increased emphasis on efficiency is coupled with reducing the numbers of employees. It would be fair to say that the primary task of the OD project has changed from 'increasing organisational effectiveness for productivity and production' to 'coping with rationalisation, redundancy, and attempting to maintain organisational effectiveness'.

Outline of the Design of the OD Scheme

A three-phase development strategy was mounted for all employees with managerial responsibility. This was to affect about 1,000 of the 3,000 people on the site, down to and including shift foreman. Decisions on vertical and horizontal cut-off points were made by top management, using cost criteria. An initial budget of about £ 70,000 was envisaged.

Phase A consisted of short seminars to help develop some basic concepts about organisational behaviour — attitudes, perception, motivation, learning, change, group work, etc.

Phase B consisted of one-week laboratories using group dynamics to develop increased awareness and adaptability in relating to others.

Phase C is an open-ended change programme worked out by managers and groups in whatever ways were relevant to their particular problems.

In summary form, the design was as follows:

	Phase A	Phase B	Phase C
Aims	concepts in organisational behaviour	skills of managerial and interpersonal work	change to improve current working
Length	3 days	5 days	ongoing
Location	off-site, non-residential	off-site, non-residential	on-site
Membership	24 managers, horizontal sample	24 managers, diagonal sample	as determined by nature of problems
Methods	lecture/seminar	group training	team development
Staff role	teachers	group process consultants	OD process consultants

The main assumption underlying this design is that the degree of confrontation relevant to the company situation should start low and build up — as people gain more awareness and confidence in the area of OD. This applies to the dimensions:

concepts – skills – change;

3 days – 5 days – indefinite;

horizontal sample – diagonal sample – work group;

teachers – process consultants – OD process consultants.

This was felt to start where the client was (anxious, training-oriented, dependent, low risk taking) and move to where the client might be able to face and deal with problems in the organisational units.

By June 1972, the planned programme of educational phases A and B were completed. It is possible that a small number of educational programmes will be designed and run to meet particular needs in servicing the phase C work. The scale of the operation is shown in the numbers of participants:

	Phase A	Phase B
Senior managers	50	53
Middle managers	116	105
Technologists, etc.	215	186
Foremen and supervisors	581	506
Totals	962	850
Number of courses	40	42

The number of senior managers on phase B is greater than the number on phase A, because some managers regarded the pilot scheme as their phase A course. Some of the numbers could be quoted as higher than those shown, because these figures refer to people who have taken part in courses and are still employed. About 20 managers who took part in phases A or B have subsequently left the company.

The question of the evaluation of the OD scheme was raised many times with senior management. Responses by them included possible surveys by personnel department, possibility of setting-up a working party, and the notion that admitting a need to evaluate the scheme showed lack of commitment! The internal consultants pressed for an evaluation by line management in terms of the impact of the scheme on actual operations. In fact, the senior management feeling prevailed and no explicit evaluation has been carried out.

Phase B Programmes

It is intended to focus on more detailed aspects of the design and operation of the phase B programmes because these involved group training methods. The context outlined above should be regarded as the environment from which participants were drawn, and to which they returned, as well as the background within which the group training was undertaken.

Over the 42 programmes, mostly with three groups of about 8 managers per programme, the design has changed considerably. The stimuli for change can be considered under headings of staff, participants, and current organisational issues.

Staff

The staff for each course has commonly consisted of one link member and two or more visiting trainers. The link members are the central team of internal and external consultants. It is the role of the link member to manage the boundary between the particular phase B programme and the larger scheme of which it is a part. The training and backgrounds of the link members differ considerably. This heterogeneity is a source of ideas and creativity, but also brings some problems of managing differences.

In all, over 20 visiting trainers have worked on the project, and each has made some impact on the design. Most of the visiting staff were already experienced group trainers or consultants, but again with widely differing approaches.

The main differences in both central and visiting staff can be traced to early differences in group work approaches. An oversimplification which is useful in identifying some of the differences is to consider a T-group/Tavistock dichotomy. (Note: The Tavistock Centre have had no direct involvement in this project. The author simply wishes to acknowledge primary sources of influence on the work, whilst full responsibility for the designs and operations involved must lie with the project team.) The T-group (6) approach tends towards interpersonal and group dynamics issues whereas the Tavistock (5, 11) approach tends to be more interpretive and intergroup-centred. Whilst conceptually there have been interactions between these major approaches, operationally many trainers have been trained from only one approach and hence their work is very much based on that style. The impact of encounter (12) group work and systems (10) thinking in organisations adds colour to the spectrum of approaches.

The initial strategy of the central team was based on an amalgamation of their personal approaches; one based on T-groups, one based on therapy groups, and one based on assumption-centred groups. Not only was this range too great, but it became increasingly apparent that a development of the assumption-centred approach was more appropriate to organisational development work, whereas the other approaches may be more relevant in personal development work. An additional factor was that the senior internal consultant had a personal preference for this approach and used his positional authority to resolve differences. Later in the project, the central team changed to reflect this development and to link more closely with the phase C work. The phase C consultancy style was based on systems (10) concepts, and external consultancy help was gained from the Grubb Institute of Behavioural Sciences (who are very strongly Tavistock-based in their approach).

Participants

The participants for phase B programmes constituted a diagonal sample of management in the organisation. Different levels were present, in proportions similar to those in the organisation, but as far as possible direct boss-subordinate pairs were avoided within groups. The participants were nominated by line management. The OD project manager informed the line managers of the dates of planned phase B courses and the kinds of numbers of staff which would be appropriate from their departments. In some departments, the scheduling of people through the courses was delegated to a clerk and at best was done so as not to clash with holiday arrangements or shift rotas. In other departments, full discussions were held to examine training needs and the relevance of phase B.

At the end of the phase A courses, and through on-the-job contact, managers were asked to discuss with their bosses and other relevant staff, their involvement in phase B. They were asked to focus on one or more current organisational problem to consider their own training needs in relation to such problems. Precourse documents also emphasised the need to think about why one was coming onto phase B and what were the learning aims. It soon became apparent that the majority of participants, particularly at the lower levels – who were the greater proportion anyway – did not work in this way. They came on the courses because they had been instructed to do so, by their bosses.

At a fairly early stage, a strong mythology grew up in the organisation about phase B. This informal system affected people's expectations much more than the attempted formal procedure. Because of the experiential nature of the programmes, people who were asked to discuss their experience with others who were now scheduled to attend, reverted to a 'wait-and-see-for-yourself' response. This gave the courses an air of secrecy and mystery. The kind of reports which were forthcoming tended to focus on the highlights of the week for that particular man. Stories of people losing their tempers, being brainwashed, being embarrassed, having their defenses stripped away, getting upset, swearing, etc., began to flourish in the atmosphere of mystery. A common predisposition was: 'Sit tight, enjoy the free food and beer, and wait and see.' Another piece of mythology which proved particularly self-fulfilling was: 'Nothing much happens until Wednesday.'

It would seem that the anxiety initially detected in the start-up of the project was fairly widespread and the OD team did not cope with this aspect very well. Data on the mythology and expectations of participants, together with numerical data showing that some departments were scheduling their members through the courses much more slowly than others, were fed back to the line management system. This attempt to confront managers with the reasons why staff were being sent on the phase B courses had little positive result.

Organisational Issues

The impact of current organisational issues and concerns has been of two kinds. One kind is based on a reaction to the courses, the other is the way the courses have been subject to tensions which already existed in the organisation.

As an example of the first kind of issue, there was some impact on the design, in the early stages, from the reactions of a few key senior managers based on their own experience and in some cases projected onto the organisation. One key manager found his own managerial style questioned by others so directly that he reacted after the course by trying to reduce the impact of the courses. He wanted shorter more highly structured programmes. The only concession which was made was to reduce the working day slightly and remove the free periods. Another very senior manager came to the conclusion, based on his own personal experience, that the courses put too much pressure on senior managers and that top managers were at special risk in this situation. It could be shown that all managers were at risk in the sense that was being used, that is to say, exposed to feedback from other managers as to their interpersonal skills. What was new was that in normal organisational life, senior managers could examine the behaviour of more junior staff but not the reverse. Whilst no actual programme changes were made to cope with this issue, the preparation of senior managers was improved and their particular problems in the course were responded to.

The other kind of organisational issue had more direct effects on the design. At one stage, a dispute developed between the company and a white collar union over compensation for overtime worked on the phase B courses by supervisory staff. The heart of the dispute was that the company did not recognise the union and refused to negotiate on the grounds that negotiation gave recognition. The union recognised the high importance being given to the OD scheme and wished to use this as a good test case to force the recognition issue. The company policy was not to compensate (in cash or time off) for overtime worked on training courses beyond the normal finishing time of 4.30 p.m. Furthermore, the company claimed that if the union advised members not to attend such courses, it would indicate that the unions were not in favour of personal and management development for its members. For a number of courses, about half the participants walked out at 4.30 p.m. and the courses became a pressure point between the company and the union. In order to cope with this issue, it was necessary to devise a design which did not collude with either side. The individual junior manager was being forced to choose between the union (and as part of that choice refuse the opportunity of management developement) and the company, which involved accepting the delay of recognition and establishment of unions for supervisory staff. The choice was between management development and union development. A new element in the design was introduced. From 4.30 p.m., the community was asked to form special interest groups and work on those special interests. Thus the members who wished to leave were also forming and working as special interest groups. At the beginning of each day, the groups checked out the feelings and implications in this matter and useful learning about shift handover and management succession issues resulted. (In this company, 24-hour 7-day-week working gives rise to frequent shift handovers, and the top management are changing jobs every two years because of the nature of the management career development policy of the international parent company.) After a few courses with this design, the situation changed as the union allowed more free choice to its members and more of them stayed beyond 4.30 p.m. The special interest groups were retained for some further courses and developed into an intergroup exercise. In course reviews and follow-up work, it became apparent that the intergroup aspects of the course were very useful and relevant to working problems; so the intergroup element in the design has been further developed.

In the later stages of the scheme, the 'business rationalisation' climate in the organisation began to generate a rather depressed atmosphere in the phase B programmes. The courses also had less participants at a senior level. This was partly because they had attended earlier courses in a higher proportion than would have been representative of the organisation, so that they could find out what the courses were about before sending their subordinate staff. The depression climate had different effects related to the responses of the different trainers. One reacted with anger, another with depression, and another with sympathy. At best, the issue was taken as a managerial problem in itself, and at least, the groups switched to a personal development strategy on the basis that even if the individual were to become redundant, he should still develop his own skill and potential (perhaps even more so).

Amongst the many participants, a small number of women were scheduled to come to the courses. The nature of the organisation was such that not only were women managers in a minority, but they were also regarded as being in less important jobs than the line managers, e.g. supervisors of administrative services, canteens, sick bay, etc. To help cope with these issues, a number of women trainers were included in the team, and normally when women participants were attending a course, women trainers were also scheduled for that course. This helped to confront the assumptions which are made concerning authority and women in managerial positions – which, in turn, was only a further example of assumptions affecting organisational behaviour independent of the task issues.

Sample Programme

The course programme continually changed over the 42 courses, particularly in the earlier stages of the scheme. As an example of a fairly stable design used for courses in the 30–35 series the following sample programme is shown.

	Monday	Tuesday	Wednesday	Thursday	Friday
09.00–10.30	introduction SG plenary		SG	SG	SG
coffee					
11.00–12.30	SG	LG	LG	LG	SG
lunch	(s.m.)				
13.45–15.00	LG	SG	SG	SG	plenary
tea					
15.15–16.30	SG	IG	IG	IG	SG
tea					
17.00–18.15	(s.m.)	IG	IG	IG plenary	(s.m.)
dinner					
19.45–21.00		IG	IG	(s.m.)	
		(s.m.)	(s.m.)		

SG = small group; LG = large group; IG = intergroup activity; (s.m.) = closed staff meetings.
There are two tea breaks in the afternoon as an aftermath of the '4.30' dispute discussed previously.
Introduction starts in plenary but moves to SG after about half-an-hour.
IG plenary is community reviewing the IG event.
Plenary on Friday is community reviewing the whole course.

Small Group

The participants were allocated to 3 groups, each with about 8 members and 1 or 2 trainers. The group composition was heterogeneous on variables of status, age, length of service, department, etc., and the groups were thus similar to one another.

The task of the small group was stated as 'to explore the behaviour of the members as it happens'. This was outlined in the precourse documents and restated in the introduction. The role of the staff was stated as 'process consultants'. These small groups formed a key reference group for participants, particularly on the earlier courses. They operated in ways closely related to T-groups with the exception that 'here-and-now' learning was occasionally checked back against analogous organisational issues. This meant that application work was not left until a 're-entry' phase at the end of the course, but was done as the group went along. In later programmes, the small groups were less salient and were used more to check out the learning gained in the large group and intergroup work, by sharing and comparing members' feelings and reactions.

The small group learning themes have tended to focus on:
− leadership needs and behaviour;
− authority and control;
− relationship between assumption-centred and task-centred work;
− confrontation and resolution, managing differences;
− helping and supporting relationships;
− feedback and the use of feelings.

The staff role has been to:
− develop a 'here-and-now' approach;
− help look at behaviour and emotions in relation to the task;
− make occasional conceptual and diagnostic inputs;
− use one's own feelings and experience in the group;
− confront the group with evidence and behaviour in the group;
− help link 'here-and-now' experience to analogous organisational issues;
− help focus on phase C, later in the week.

Trainer interventions have been concerned with group operation, interpersonal relations, and assumptions (5). They are not concerned with the topic under discussion, even where the topic is the behaviour in the group, nor are they concerned with personal or therapeutic issues. The main focus is on what people do with what they are, not how they came to be that way, or whether that is a 'good' way to be.

The trainer problems encountered in the small group work have included:

(a) Confusion between application work and flight (e.g. 'this is the kind of thing which keeps happening at work'), which could be a useful check of relevance and importance of the topic under discussion; or it could be an attempt to get out of the group 'here-and-now' work and generalise about back-home matters.

(b) Interpretation and diagnosis precipitate, if not cause, counterdependency; which is then in turn interpreted. There is always strong pressure in the group towards dependency due to the authoritarian climate from which participants come and the anxiety of coping, without technology as the main reference point. The trainer needs to be able to work through the group/trainer relationship satisfactorily if useful work is to follow on authority issues.

(c) Many participants feel deskilled, when they are asked to operate with their managerial skills but without their technological expertise. This can develop into the assumption that the purpose of the course is to make people feel lost or inadequate, which in turn leads to the assumption that feedback equals criticism. A significant number of participants reported a loss of confidence during and after the courses — which is contrary to one of the aims of the OD project.

Large Group

The large group is the total community working together in one room. The stated purpose is to examine members' behaviour in a situation where it is not possible for each person to maintain interpersonal relationships with every other person. The room is arranged to seat all participants and staff in two or three concentric circles, facing inwards. This means that some members cannot see or be seen by other members. Centrality and power take on physical meanings and the effect is to heighten the issues related to the stated purpose. The large group is intended to simulate in a learning climate some of the problems of working in a large organisation. In terms of current large group training methodology, the group size of 24 (plus staff) is not really very large. It should more accurately be termed a median group, but is the largest which can be mustered, and the fact that all participants come from the same large organisation (in a diagonal sample) does seem to help produce useful large group dynamics.

The learning themes of the large group have included:
— individuality and identity in a large organisation;
— identification and use of resources;
— risk-taking and the use of initiative;
— authority and control;
— decision-making in large groups;
— fight/flight, pairing, dependency;
— growth of fantasy and mythology;
— managing differences in the amount of participation;
— operation of power elites and subgroups;
— attempts to cope with organisational problems by changing layout and structure.

The last item on this list refers to a fairly consistent tendency for participants to react to the difficulty of working as a large group by blaming the seating layout, which the staff have arranged (opportunity to test authority issues), and experiment by moving the chairs into one large circle.

The staff role is somewhat similar to small group process consultancy but is more demanding in some aspects:
— trainer has to cope with identity problems, and several other trainers;
— trainers are seen as a key power elite group;
— models and concepts of large group dynamics are different from small group work;
— differences of trainers styles are seen openly, and interact.

Intergroup

The intergroup activity involves all members of the community and its purpose is to focus on behaviour between groups and individual behaviour in crossing group boundaries. The community is asked, in an introductory plenary on the afternoon of the second day, to form itself into new groups to work towards the stated purpose. There is an implication in the task and its introduction that movement between groups will be necessary for experiential learning. In some courses, the whole community has also been given the task of planning and running the intergroup review plenary which is scheduled for the afternoon of the fourth day.

The staff operate as a group, offering process consultancy services in the community – but only on intergroup issues, not intragroup work.

The learning themes of the intergroup event include:
– definition, nature, and maintenance of group boundaries;
– individual roles in relation to boundary management;
– crossing group boundaries, joining and leaving;
– co-operation and competition between groups;
– co-ordination of several groups with a common purpose;
– intergroup stereotypes and mythology;
– establishing integrative functions and structures;
– use of service groups, including OD consultants.

Many of the comments made about the staff role in small and large groups apply to the intergroup activity, with the additional factor that concepts and skills in intergroup work (9, 10) are needed. In particular, the staff need to maintain clarity of role, if precedents about the work of OD consultants for phase C are being set.

Staff Meetings

Staff meetings were of two forms. Short informal discussions during meal breaks were useful for quick 'checking-out' and support. Some trainers found this useful in helping release tensions which they had been unable to work with in the group! Reviewing and planning meetings were also held, usually at the end of each day. These are shown on the sample programme and were shown on the programme available to members. Most courses had closed staff meetings. For a short series, about one-third of the way through the project, the staff experimented with open staff meetings at the suggestion of a new visiting trainer. Participants were allowed to attend the planned staff meetings to observe. An empty chair was included in the meeting so that participants who wished to say something could join the meeting on a temporary basis and later leave again. This degree of control was felt necessary to limit the participation of non-staff members so that the primary task of the staff meeting could be pursued.

The main problem encountered with open staff meetings was that they became major trainer interventions into large group and intergroup work, as well as providing a link between small groups, and staff had some difficulty in handling this aspect. The advantages were felt to be in possibilities of reducing unrealistic fantasies about what the staff talked about, which could develop in the minds of participants. Often the open staff meeting would be followed by an informal closed meeting in the staff-only bar — which is evidence that the staff were having difficulty saying all that they wished to say in an open meeting. With further different visiting trainers, the disadvantages seemed to outweigh the advantages and a return was made to closed staff meetings.

Staff Development

The original nucleus of consultants was expanded by inviting additional visiting trainers. All additional staff were experienced group trainers, but with great variety in their backgrounds and approaches. Each visiting trainer was asked first to co-train with a member of the central group. The purpose of the co-training was twofold. Firstly, to orient additional staff to the philosophy of the phase B courses and the whole OD scheme. Secondly, to evaluate their potential suitability for further work on these programmes. Some co-trainers did not proceed further, whilst others became part of the regular pool of additional trainers, and a few became part of the nucleus group and co-trained with further new staff in turn.

It was important to face the difference between 'doing your own thing', which is a luxury we are sometimes afforded in one—off open stranger labs, and training as part of an ongoing OD project. In this project, many groups were run (about 124 in all) and in the middle and later stages, a degree of consistency of design and approach had been established. Whilst further work needed to be sensitive to new issues arising in the particular community, it also needed to be in line with previous courses if participants were to work after the course with others who had attended earlier or later programmes. A written outline of the nature of the phase B design was used to help orient additional staff who were coping with a boundary crossing problem of their own. The way they coped with this issue was useful insight into their potential for the intergroup event. The autonomy of the staff group for any one phase B was fairly limited. In each staff group, the member of the central team had specific responsibility for managing the boundary between that course and the whole operation. The controls on visiting staff were felt to be too constraining by some trainers who, after all, had considerable experience already; but the issue remained that trainers were not being told how to work, they were being asked to work in such a way that that would be consistent and compatible with the overall project. The majority of the visiting staff were able to have some influence on the design and were able to retain the basis of their own training style. In return for any constraints, they felt that they also learned from the differences in approach and design.

The later phase B design is somewhat demanding on staff resources. The design calls for group training skills with ongoing application work, large group skills, and intergroup process consultancy skills. For this reason, there has been a shift towards the 'Tavistock' end of the 'Tavistock/T-group' spectrum. Without wishing to imply nationalistic biases, it may be fair to reflect that the spectrum could also be regarded as 'British/American', or institutionally as 'Tavistock/NTL'.

A useful by-product of this project is that considerable impact has been made on a significant number of trainers through their involvement in these courses.

Impact and Results

The impact and effectiveness of the phase B courses should be assessed in the phase C activities. The 'proof of the pudding' is not in the eating, it is in the nutritional or indigestive effects afterwards!

However, one phase B programme was researched directly, and before dealing with the phase C impact, this research can be dealt with briefly. The research was a pilot project prior to a research project planned to measure the effects of changing to a residential design for the phase B courses. In the event, the cutback of finance throughout the company meant that no residential programmes could be run because of the high additional cost — independent of any benefits which may have been gained. Data were collected by questionnaires before and after the course, and by tape recordings taken in the small group sessions on Tuesday and Thursday. Analysis focussed on changes in self-concept, self-acceptance, task/process concern, trainer assessments, and attitudes to leadership. Useful data were generated on managerial styles by combining some of these variables. The most significant independent variables which could be identified as possible sources of the shifts were trainer style and group composition. This is hardly surprising or original, since most of the research on T-groups (7) has focussed on these two issues. It does demonstrate that research is feasible on industrial programmes (most research seems to be with student participants or with open laboratories) and could be a useful contribution to course development.

The key issue in considering the impact of phase B upon phase C is essentially whether there is any impact or not. It is not very meaningful to consider whether the impact is as intended or not, because at this stage there are no clear intentions as to how the organisation should change as a whole — these have to be worked out for each section as phase C begins to get under way.

A high proportion of participants, about 50 %, have not become involved in any projects which could be classed as phase C, or traced to the stimulus of phase B. This could be due to a number of factors, even assuming that there was some learning on phase B:

(a) An organisation of some 3,000 people is more than able to cope with the output of each separate phase B course – dynamic conservatism at work. Some seed falls on stony ground, some is shifted to stony ground after it falls, and much is choked by the surrounding weeds.

(b) Early phase B participants felt the lack of others who had experience of this kind of work as ground for mutual support. They waited for more colleagues to come through the system. Later participants saw that earlier members had done little as yet, so why should they?

(c) Many participants were sent by middle and senior management who were either not committed to the OD scheme or were actually against it. These managers sent their subordinates because top management expected them to do so; but they made it clear to their subordinates, by various subtle signs, that they should not entertain any ideas about change or development.

In the case of managers who have become involved in phase C type-activities, at least two important factors other than phase B are operating. One is the effect of organisational and attitudinal changes related to the current 'business rationalisation' syndrome. This has given rise to structural changes, promotions and redundancies, and a clear need to demonstrate efficiency. Some managers have used their phase B impetus to help them cope with these issues, and others have started some phase C work in the hope that it demonstrates their willingness to pursue organisational efficiency.

The other main factor operating is the support network operating and, in particular, the work of the internal OD consultants. The internal consultants have for some time had more requests for help with on-the-job development work than they can properly cope with. Some of their time is taken up as members of the nucleus team for phase B work, some in managing the overall phase A-B-C system, and some in personal and professional development for themselves. This has necessitated the setting of priorities and criteria for deciding which requests for help to respond to, and how to allocate resources. Some, but not much, external consultancy resource has been used on phase C work, but the nature of the work lends itself more to full-time internal consultants. Some managers have been identified as key people in influencing developments in particular areas. These managers have been followed-up, responded to more readily. There was also felt to be a need to work through a small number of successful phase C projects to be completed so that the organisation could see the positive results of OD and share the learning across departments. This is also related to the need for internal consultants to demonstrate their competence and helpfulness in order to establish this role as a viable service to line management and not just another luxury idea of the personnel department.

The basic conclusion has to be that the phase B activities have generated at least more phase C work than can be coped with, given the scale of resources. This is evidence of the impact of phase B, but also reflects a basic flaw in the original scheme design in that too much effort has been placed in training and too little in on-the-job support. This is partly a strategic error on the part of the original external consultants and partly related to the training bias in the company, and many other companies, which has been discussed earlier. The implication is that some of the phase B effort has been wasted because it produced potential development, not all of which could be followed-up.

The main phase C activities which have been supported have been most useful. The internal consultants are able to demonstrate several successful projects in key areas of the business.

In addition to the direct impact on the main manufacturing unit concerned in this project, there have been some wider implications in the company. The project has been closely observed by both the parent company and other units — as one way of tackling OD work. Another unit with close operational ties with the one concerned has entered into some OD activities of a similar form but with changes based on lessons learned in this project. Within the vicinity of the main unit, a research and development unit is currently creating an OD strategy.

Discussion

The most significant aspects of this case study in the use of group training in organisational development are:
 — the scale of the project;
 — integrating diverse approaches to group training;
 — influence of the organisation on the training work;
 — impact of the training on the organisation.

These aspects are interactive. Only in a large-scale project is it possible to work with the diversity of approaches and work through the design and application problems. In general, it is only large commercial organisations which can afford to mount such projects, and are currently doing so in the name of OD. In such cases, the organisation should determine the nature of the training and the training is intended to have effects in the organisation.

Considering the phase B system as a part of a wider OD system, it is clear that phase B operated as an open system (8):
 — importation of energy: participants and staff, organisational experience;
 — throughput: the activities in the course, behaviour and learning processes;
 — output: participants to phase C, trainer experience;
 — cycles of events: the programme with cycles of small and large groups and intergroups;

— negative entropy: continued attempts to make sense of experience;

— information, feedback, coding: attempts to conceptualise and share experience;

— dynamic homeostasis: development of a live but stable design;

— differentiation: separate learning issues in small and large groups and intergroups;

— equifinality: it is likely that similar results could have been achieved by other means and training methods.

By looking at the phase B activities in this way, one is reminded of the dependence of the phase B system on the inputs from wider systems. This means that variations in the input, such as participants' attitudes and trainers' ideas, are a source of energy and are not error variances. For example, when the 'business rationalisation' syndrome first developed, the participants were depressed. The initial reaction of the training staff was to complain that participants were not as good as they used to be! This suggests that the danger of regarding the running of courses as central, and participants' attitudes as a constraint, was being encountered.

The scale of the project could have increased the danger that a production line for trainees became established, independent of the needs of the organisation or the purpose of the training within the whole project.

The implications of integrating various approaches to group training within the design could be far-reaching. It would seem useful to differentiate learning goals and issues, but partisan to differentiate according to approaches to training held by different staff members. It is likely that the individual group trainer sees his or her own experience and the approach developed in this experience as a special contribution which they can make to the programme. However, in approaching a client system and in working out a design, these contributions need to be assessed in terms of relevance and effectiveness. Many trainers are trained by institutions or networks which are parochial and incestuous. The manager of a subsystem like phase B, and the person on each course with responsibility for boundary management between that course and the larger system, has a difficult task in helping the staff group work in such a way that decisions are based on evidence of relevance and effectiveness of methods and not on prejudice.

The dangers of a single approach include the notion of group training as a panacea for organisational problems. With the concept of equifinality in mind, it may be that any one of a member of approaches will achieve basically the same result, but once a system is operating, equifinality does not mean that optimistic guesswork will be a sufficient substitute for feedback and control. It would be an exaggeration, but not a big exaggeration, to believe that some trainers start with their preferred approach and then seek the most suitable clients. To balance the argument somewhat, it is better that trainers should do what they are reasonably good at — in the sense that a good T-group may be better than a bad large

---

group experience, even for issues which would more appropriately be tackled by a good large group event.

The problem remains that even the intention to be inclusive in choice of methods and approaches, and client-centred, is not enough. It is still difficult to check if one is really doing this or simply rationalising prejudices anyway.

Yet another interesting factor in using group training within a larger project is that the network of trainers operates in such a way that sentient links play at least as much a part as the task systems. One such factor is reciprocity between trainers. The sentient links can have a beneficial effect, particularly when the system is managed with some clarity about task and sentient systems (10).

An important conclusion which cannot be overemphasised in this case study of group training in OD is that the internal consultants are a key factor in the success or failure of the project. They provide the vital link between the current themes and issues in the organisation as well as the feedback links as to the effects of the training. Most important of all, they carry out the essential follow-up work without which much of the training would be wasted. It is possible to fulfil some of these functions without having full-time internal consultants in the organisation, but the commitment which internal people have to the success of the organisation does seem to be beneficial. External consultants and visiting trainers are useful not only in providing ideas and resources but in providing a support system for the internal staff. It would also appear that, financially, internal resources are less expensive than continued hiring of external people. However, the establishment of internal resources is probably the biggest single factor which distinguishes OD from training.

Acknowledgements

The author accepts responsibility for the views, opinions, and information in this paper, but wishes to acknowledge the important part played in the project by: *Michael Armstrong, Trevor Mumby, Charles Cox,* and the many visiting trainers without whom the project would not have been completed to this stage. All these people, together with the managers who took part in the courses and discussions, have helped me to an extent that I feel the whole project was designed to train me.

References

1   *Argyris, C.:* Intervention theory and method – a behavioural science view (Addison-Wesley, Massachusetts 1970).
2   *Bennis, W.G.:* Organisation development – its nature, origins, and prospects (Addison-Wesley, Massachusetts 1970).

3   *Bennis, W.G.; Benne, K.D., and Chin, R.:* The planning of change (Holt, Rinehart & Winston, New York 1969).
4   *Beckhard, R.:* Organisation development – strategies and models (Addison-Wesley, Massachusetts 1969).
5   *Bion, W.R.:* Experiences in groups – and other papers (Tavistock, London 1961).
6   *Bradford, L.P.; Gibb, J.R., and Benne, K.D. (ed.):* T-group theory and laboratory method (Wiley, New York 1964).
7   *Cooper, C.L. and Mangham, I.L. (ed.):* T-groups – a survey of research (Wiley-Interscience, London 1971).
8   *Katz, D. and Kahn, R.L.:* The social psychology of organisations (Wiley, New York 1966).
9   *Lawrence, P.R. and Lorsch, J.W.:* Developing organisations – diagnosis and action (Addison-Wesley, Massachusetts 1969).
10 *Miller, E.J. and Rice, A.K.:* Systems of organisation – the control of task and sentient boundaries (Tavistock, London 1967).
11 *Rice, A.K.:* Learning for leadership (Tavistock, London 1965).
12 *Rogers, C.R.:* Encounter groups (Allen Lane, London 1971).
13 *Schein, E.H.:* Process consultation – its role in organisation development (Addison-Wesley, Massachusetts 1969).
14 *Schein, E.H. and Bennis, W.G.:* Personal and organisational change through group methods (Wiley, New York 1965).

Author's address: *Kenneth Harrison*, Department of Management Sciences, University of Manchester Institute of Science and Technology, P.O. Box 88, Sackville Street, *Manchester 1* (England)

Interpers. Develop. *3:* 100–114 (1972)

Group Training for Community Relations
The Community Workshop

K. Olmosk and G. Graversen

Department of Management Studies, University of Leeds, Leeds

In recent years, the question of how to deal with conflict and resolve community problems in multicultural settings has been of growing concern in both Europe and the United States. Old established methods for dealing with these problems are being called into question as more subgroups become militant in demanding a say in decisions affecting an increasingly pluralistic society.

Although the problems are highly complex and varied, a number of studies have indicated that group techniques can be developed which offer some hope of success in dealing with them. Studies by *Rubin* (4) and *Klein et al.* (2) have used group techniques to make issues of interracial relations explicit and to modify racial attitudes. Attempts to use group methods to resolve border conflicts in Eastern Africa (5), school-community conflicts in New York City (3), and social worker-welfare recipient relations in North Carolina (1) have also helped to clarify many of the issues involved. The programme reported here is part of a study designed to add to this growing body of knowledge.

Some Characteristics of a Community Workshop

Before going on to describe this programme, we should like to draw attention to some of the characteristics of this kind of endeavour which distinguish it from other types of laboratory training. To do this, we will compare the main features of a community workshop with those of a human relations training laboratory. The importance of these characteristics will be referred to again later in this report.

Whereas the participant in a human relations laboratory represents only himself, *the participants in community workshops represent groups in the community.* The participants are not drawn randomly from the population at large. The composition of the workshop population is determined by the groups that exist in the community who are affected by the problem to be focused on in the workshop. Thus, the individual participants may represent the police, the youth, the immigrant groups, the local government, etc. This does not mean that each has or needs any official mandate from the group that he represents, only that he identifies himself or will be identified by others as a member of an existing group in the community.

In human relations training, the target for change and development is the individual. *In community workshops, the change target is the community.* Improved intergroup relations, increased communication and contact, better community services, more influence and participation in local government, etc., are examples of objectives for community workshops. This does not exclude individual learning from the community workshops. It merely subordinates the individual learning to the goal of community development. In situations like the one studied here, attitude changes concerning racial prejudice can be a crucial part of the learning, but the main aim is to improve school-community relations.

Human relations labs are (most often) stranger labs where interdependence between the participants does not exist outside the training situation. *In community workshops, interdependence exists between the groups outside as well as inside the training situation.* It is on this interdependence that the composition of the workshop is based. The interdependence outside the training situation also makes action planning and the transfer of workshop learning to back-home situations realistically possible.

The features so far mentioned have to do with the change targets and the participants in a community workshop. They are the preconditions for the design. The design itself also differs in some important ways from those often used in human relations labs.

In human relations labs, the dynamics in the groups (T-groups) and between groups are determined only by the laboratory setting. Groups are composed randomly or deliberately 'equalized' so that preconditioned differences between groups are eliminated. The particular dynamics that emerge during the development of the lab are only predictable in general social-psychological terms and do not take the dynamics in the larger society into account, except in a very general way. *The design in community workshops, including the composition of groups, is based upon the dynamics in the community.* Developments in the workshop may change these dynamics (often this is one of the training aims), but only by acting on them, not by avoiding them. The initial situation is structured around problems that exist in the community, and the design aims at giving participants an opportunity to learn by dealing with and possibly eliminating the problems — both in the training situation and in the community.

In human relations labs, the focus is on the development of interpersonal skills, although intergroup conflict may be part of the learning situation. *The focus in community workshops is on intergroup development.* Therefore, T-groups are more likely to be subordinated to exercises designed to clarify intergroup issues in community workshops than they are in human relations labs.

Finally, *it is essential in the community workshop that action planning is part of the design.* To what extent realistic planning actually can take place varies with a number of factors (such as the influence of the participants in the community) and expectations should not be set too high. However, it is important that this part of the community workshop is not neglected as it has several functions apart from bringing about the desired changes. It establishes the fact that problems in the community can be acted upon, that different groups in the community are interdependent, and that groups in the community can work together on common problems. It also extends the commitment of the participants to the objectives of the training beyond the time limits of the workshop.

These notions concerning the basic characteristics of a community workshop provided a starting point for us in our design. Our approach combined many characteristics of a task-oriented organization development (OD) workshop with a mini-society lab.

What follows is a mixture of the events as they appeared at the time and hindsight. It is hoped that this combination will provide a reasonably complete picture of some of the problems we encountered in the following workshop, and that the picture will be illustrative of general problems in community relations training.

Background

As a result of discussions which took place during a meeting of the Group Relations Training Association in September of 1971, *Peter B. Smith* (University of Sussex), *Gert Graversen* (University of Leeds), and *Ned Levine* (Brunel University) made application to the Home Office for a research grant to study the effects of multiracial sensitivity training. It was proposed that two weekend training programmes be conducted, each of which would utilize group training techniques. One programme would be based in the north of England and the other in the southeast. The goals of both programmes would be to increase participant understanding of behaviour in multiracial settings, but the specific design of each weekend would be left to the actual training staff.

The following report is concerned only with the programme devised for the city in the north of England. A report of the larger project is in the process of being prepared.

Setting

The city chosen in the north was an industrial centre with a population of approximately one-half million. Roughly 3 % of the population is non-white and about 2 % are West Indian. The problems of the non-white community are further complicated by the fact that most of them are recent immigrants or second generation English.

One of the areas of increasing concern to West Indian parents has been the adjustment of West Indian children in the schools and the ability of the white teachers to understand their problems. Relations between parents and school authorities have often been characterized by lack of information concerning problems, suspicion and a growing sense of frustration. Although the situation is not yet critical, there has been a growing sense that something needs to be done.

With this situation in mind, the group from the University of Leeds, composed of *Gert Graversen, Kurt Olmosk* and *Paul Sommerfeld,* proposed a teacher-parent workshop on the problems of black children in schools. We hoped that by bringing a number of parents and teachers together, and using group training techniques to help them discuss their mutual concerns, a core group could be established to continue working on community problems.

Organization and Pre-Planning

The staff for the workshop met early in December 1971 to design the weekend for the programme. At the first meeting, the general approach to the workshop (outlined earlier as characteristics of a community workshop) was agreed. Decisions were also made concerning which segments of the community to approach and how participants were to be recruited. It seemed at the time that we had reached agreement on all of the major issues. Later events indicated that this was not the case.

Although we had basically agreed on a community problem-solving approach with an OD emphasis, one of us saw interpersonal learning and growth as an extremely important part of this and another was primarily concerned with improving the conditions for the children in the schools. These differences were later resolved, but point up how easily confusion can occur in this type of project.

Throughout the project, it was also necessary to remember that the workshop was a part of a larger research study. Although this did not alter the design of the workshop, it imposed some time constraints on us. It was necessary to allow enough time for all participants to be interviewed before the programme. It also made it more difficult to recruit participants since they were committing themselves to several hours of interviews as well as to the weekend workshop.

Recruiting Participants

Once the Home Office had approved the funding for the project, we contacted the city's Education Department informing them of our intentions to hold the workshop and asking for their cooperation. This was soon forthcoming.

Through the Education Department, we secured the cooperation of the headmasters of three schools; one county primary school, one county secondary school, and one comprehensive school. The headmasters agreed to support our programme by talking to the teachers at their schools about our programme and asking interested parties to attend a meeting with the workshop organizers. All teachers who participated were to be volunteers. It was important, however, particularly to the teachers, that our project had official sanctions.

On February 1, 1972 the workshop organizers met with those interested teachers at one of the schools. At this meeting, we explained the purposes and general design of the workshop and the proposed research.

During the meeting, considerable scepticism and suspicion concerning the goals and methods of the workshop were expressed. With hindsight, this appears to have been an attempt to test the sincerity and competence of the staff rather than actual hostility toward the idea of the workshop. The willingness of the staff to share their own concerns as well as their hopes and plans went a long way toward allaying any doubts the teachers may have had. By the end of this meeting, the teachers had agreed to accept much of the responsibility for contacting parents and inviting them to participate in the programme.

The majority of parents were recruited by the teachers. A few were recruited through the community relations officer with whom we had previous contact. Once the parents expressed an interest in the project, they received, by mail, a two-page description of the aims and methods to be used in the workshop. This was followed by the researcher contacting them and arranging for interviews.

We were initially somewhat concerned that approaching the parents in this way would mean that the teachers would recruit only those parents they already knew and who were already quite active in the schools. This proved not to be that case. Many of the parents had very little contact with the teachers prior to the workshop, and seemed to be a reasonable cross-section of West Indian parents from the schools involved.

The workshop opened with 13 parents and 14 teachers from three different schools. We had decided to try to get several parents and teachers from each of two or three schools, rather than to get one or two participants from a larger number of schools. This decision was made in order to increase our chances of generating some lasting change in the community; by helping participants to provide support and encouragement to each other after the workshop.

Arrangements for the Workshop

All arrangements for the workshop were made and paid for by the organizers. The weekend was residential and began with dinner on Friday, 25 February. The site which had been chosen was a retreat house about 20 miles from the city. The arrangements were not luxurious but there were good meeting rooms, spacious grounds and enough sleeping rooms so that participants could be housed two to a room. The workshop ended at approximately 4.30 p.m. Sunday afternoon, 27 February.

Workshop Design

The goals of the workshop, as stated in the description sent to all participants before the workshop, were as follows:
To help black parents and white teachers to
(1) increase their awareness of the breadth and depth of interracial problems facing primary and secondary schools in their community;
(2) learn about and understand the individual and cultural perspectives of the other;
(3) understand their own attitudes and behaviour with respect to school problems by being confronted with alternative perspectives;
(4) increase their communications concerning school problems;
(5) begin planning action steps toward alleviating some of these problems. These goals provided the direction for the following design:

Workshop design

Phase I – getting acquainted – climate setting

Friday evening	Discussion in small groups with changing group composition	Focus: Introduce self, explore expectations, hopes and goals for the weekend

Phase II – identifying and working on problem areas

Saturday morning	Homogeneous groups	Focus: What problems do we have in relating to the other group (parents/teachers)?
	General session	Focus: Confrontation and sharing of perceptions
	Small cross groups	Focus: Elaboration of issues raised
Saturday afternoon	Homogeneous groups	Focus: Which issues do we want to deal with during the rest of the weekend?
	General session	Focus: Begin work on issues raised

| Saturday evening | General session | Focus: Continue work on issues raised |
| Sunday morning (first half) | Small cross groups | Focus: Obtain some closure on issues raised |

Phase III — action planning

Sunday morning (second half)	Small cross groups	Focus: Identify action steps
	General session	Focus: Reports of action steps identified; decisions on timing and responsibility for making sure action is taken
Sunday afternoon	General session	Focus: Close of workshop

Initial Outcomes

In general, the workshop seems to have met most of the stated objectives. Data collected after the workshop would indicate that both teachers and parents felt they had a better understanding of the problems facing the schools and had deepened their commitment to trying to solve these problems.

As a direct result of the workshop, a number of other events have taken place. The quotation below, written by one of the teachers who attended the workshop, gives some idea of a few of these:

'... it was agreed that the County Primary school should institute a parents night, the mission of which would be to give West Indian parents an insight into the running of the school and perhaps allay parental fears about certain aspects of their children's education. We were delighted to hear that Mrs. ————, a parent, would be closely connected with the organization of the evening and that Miss ———— (the Headmistress) would accept responsibility for informing local primary junior schools of her intentions and would try to encourage them into organizing equivalent activities ...

'... the Chairman of the Education Committee be asked about the possibility of immigrant parents being invited to serve on the proposed Board of Governors. Since this meeting, Alderman ———— has expressed a desire to attend the meeting to be held on March 28th.

'... It is undeniable that the workshop will have far-reaching consequences. By coincidence, a parents evening, in which West Indian parents were invited to meet senior staff of ———— had already been organized. The evening was extremely well attended and was successful, there being refreshing frankness on both sides. It is my belief that its success was in part due to the ambassadorial work done by teachers and parents who had attended the workshop.

'I am sure that other schools will be working along similar lines so it may be profitable in this report to itemize the activities to which one school has committed itself. These are:

(a) to devise a system whereby staff and parents can get to know each other as people: this system will be experimented with in summer term;

(b) to organize more parents evenings;

(c) to find a method by which parents could see the school under normal operating conditions;

(d) to organize an International evening to foster good relationships between the area's several ethnic groups;

(e) to attempt a reform of the PTA so that many more parents, particularly West Indian parents, are involved.'

Just how long the effects of the workshop will last only time will tell. The longer research study, of which this project is a part, should give some indication. The initial reactions do indicate that even a comparatively short workshop can have a much larger impact.

Issues in Community Workshops

Before closing this paper, we would like to present what we believe to be some of the major issues in running this type of workshop.

Staff Planning

The staff for this workshop had at least five planning meetings and were in fairly regular contact before it took place. Even so, there was some difference in outlook regarding the hoped for outcomes of the workshop. As we mentioned earlier, these did not become major problems because they were recognized fairly early in the actual workshop and the staff had built the kind of relationships which allowed the issue to be faced. However, it seems to us that this type of workshop requires considerably more effort to build a strong staff team and working relationships than is often expended.

Participant Selection

Bearing in mind that the change target is the community, it can be justified and is often necessary to set out some requirements for participation.

Influence. Since the workshop was designed to begin the exploration of the community issues rather than to seek final solutions, we did not feel it was critical to select participants who were particularly influential back home. In general, we would still feel this to be true. However, in order for the outcome of such a workshop to spread, it is necessary that the participants include persons who have the confidence of the groups they are chosen to represent. In a few cases, this was probably not true of participants at this workshop.

Emotion and intellect. The issues raised in the workshop were often emotionally loaded. Cultural biases and racial prejudices became evident and were often difficult to deal with. This was expected, in fact it was one of the aims of the workshop, but still caused frustration and stress. This pointed up to us the need to start with stable people as participants.

The complexity of the issues also requires that the participants be reasonably articulate. This does not mean they need to be highly educated, many of our participants were not. It does mean that they must be capable of seeing some alternative points of view and be capable of talking about these.

It is also important that the participants be willing to listen to other points of view. It is extremely easy in this type of workshop, for one member to block the entire process by insisting that there is only one possible solution to any problem or one right way to run a discussion. If this happens, the workshop is likely to generate frustration and tension within the larger community rather than helping to solve problems.

Information and interest. During the workshop, it became clear that there was considerable diversity among the participants as to the degree of interest and information concerning issues being discussed. During some discussion, several participants did not have sufficient interest in the issues to make the high level of emotional and intellectual investment required. This often led either to only partial participation of these group members or to premature attempts to close off discussion.

At other times, it became clear that some participants had considerably more information than others did. This both helped and hindered the workshop. It helped in that it broke down some of the stereotypes of each subgroup being a monolithic unit, thereby allowing some participants to begin dealing with each other as people.

It hindered the workshop in two ways. First, it made it necessary occasionally to discuss problems at a fairly low level until everybody could be brought up to date. At times this led to some participants becoming impatient with what seemed to them to be a discussion of old issues. Second, the uneven background knowledge tended to limit the ability of some participants to assess various action steps. Some of these problems could probably have been alleviated by providing all participants with background reading material in advance.

Recruiting Process

As mentioned earlier, most of the participants for this workshop were recruited through the Department of Education hierarchy, either directly or indirectly. This was necessary since without the approval of the Department of Education it is unlikely that we would have been able to recruit many teachers. It would also have severely limited the possibilities for follow-up action after the workshop. However, this method of recruiting also had some drawbacks.

Once the Department of Education had given their approval for the programme, there was a tendency for some of the participants to think of it as being run by the educational establishment. Several headmasters gave the programme their blessing and one even freed two teachers from some of their other duties for a few days to help with the recruiting of parents. This had one unforeseen repercussion.

At a meeting of one of the local black militant groups shortly before the workshop, the issue of who was in charge of the workshop was discussed. Because of relations between this group and one of the headmasters who had given his support, this group decided to boycott the workshop and several people who had agreed to participate withdrew. The dynamics behind this event were, more than anything else, suspicion about the motives and intentions of those influencing the selection of participants. As such they were indicative of the level of trust amongst parts of the community.

This problem reminded us once again that we were going to have to deal with the dynamics of the larger community during this workshop and not just with individual participants. We felt beforehand that it was important for the staff to remain politically neutral throughout the programme. Our experience would indicate that this was indeed important but very difficult to do in practice – the relationships in the larger community influence the workshop at every step on the way.

The recruitment of parents faced us with some specific problems, some of which turned out to be more imagined than real. We rejected the idea of inviting parents by letter, assuming that this was not likely to get much response. A more personal approach was called for. As the staff had little contact with the West Indian community, the teachers were the prime source of contact with the parents. The teachers themselves were sceptical about the willingness of West Indian parents to spend a weekend away from home, and had to be convinced that it was worth asking them. Their scepticism turned out not to be justified. The parents were very interested and there was a positive response to the personal approach by the teachers.

This approach to recruitment had an added benefit. Using the teachers to recruit the parents, increased the teachers commitment to the success of the project as well as increasing their contact with the community (which was one of the aims of the project).

Location
One of the issues which arose during the initial recruiting for the programme and again later at the workshop, was whether or not this workshop could have been held at one of the schools rather than at a retreat house in the country. After considerable discussion, both within the staff and with the participants, we still feel that the choice of the retreat house was a good one. None of the groups were on their own home ground. The parents in particular said that they usually felt intimidated when meeting teachers in the schools. Second, the site was sufficiently isolated that there were few family or professional distractions. This isolation allowed deeper immersion into the intellectual and emotional processes of the workshop and allowed some of the old attitudes and thought processes to be modified. However, since the outcomes of the workshop had to be sold to

other people 'back-home', the cultural island effect may have created problems of credibility.

Time Limits

The short ($2\frac{1}{2}$ days) time allowed for the workshop forced us to drastically reduce the time we would have liked to allocate to some activities. Generally, what this meant was that there was insufficient time to develop relations within each subgroup, develop the community as a whole, or allow much free time for reflection or more informal discussion.

One dilemma we faced as a staff was how much direction and 'help' to give, and how much to rely upon the organic development of a self-directed group. It was obvious that we had to take the time constraint into consideration. The functioning of the large group (30 including staff) was crucial. The ability, at least by the end of the weekend, to work as a decision-making body, with high commitment from all members, was important for the success of the workshop and the follow-up activities. For the large group to become an effective decision-making body, it needed to work through a number of issues around its own functioning. These included the behaviour and feelings of the individual members. It would no doubt have been of value if this could have been done, but considering the time limit and the main objectives of the workshop, we settled for less and compromised on the group process and development issues. We assumed responsibility for the minimum group maintenance necessary to allow the group to concentrate on task issues. In practice, this was done by the staff providing the overall structure of the workshop, and a staff member chairing each of the large meetings.

Despite the fact that a number of issues and latent problems in the group had not been worked through, the compromise was successful. The group was able to work as a self-directed unit after the workshop and to produce results.

Questions about silent members, inclusion, control, authority-dependency, and similar processes within the group, were often not brought out into the open where they could be worked on by the group. This was frustrating for at least one of the staff members who had to keep himself from digging into the process issues, the more familiar and more rewarding role for most group trainers.

Limiting the amount of time spent on processing the group also had the effect of limiting the emphasis on interpersonal relations. (The process of giving feedback in T-groups is often a means of developing intimacy amongst the group members.)

In spite of the costs, we found that our compromise was a viable solution to the problem of time limitations. In community relations training, the ability to work with such compromises seems to be necessary if one wants to reach stated goals. It is our suspicion that many community relations training programmes fail because trainers are not willing or able to compromise on their group training values.

Workshop Design

Two features of the workshop design are worth noting. These were the phases designed into the workshop and the groupings used.

Phasing. The workshop consisted of three phases. Each was conceived as having a specific focus and together they provided the framework for the weekend.

The first phase had a climate setting and unfreezing function. During this phase, participants were asked to get acquainted, share expectations, and to discuss what they felt needed to happen to make the weekend a success. Groupings were changed frequently and people were encouraged to meet each other and communicate openly.

One specific part of this phase is worth mentioning. During the last hour of Friday evening, four groups were formed and asked to discuss what they would consider a successful outcome to the weekend. During this discussion, sheets of newsprint were provided and the groups were asked to use these to keep track of the most important points in their discussion. They were also asked to be prepared to present these briefly to the total group at the end of the evening. The evening closed with a short plenary session to present this data. This worked quite well to set a tone of involvement and responsibility for the outcome of the workshop.

The second phase was designed to identify problems and to begin work on them. In general, each grouping lasted at least $1\frac{1}{2}$ hours and the whole phase was built around an intergroup confrontation model.

The third and final phase was designed around action planning. This we felt should include not only idea generation but decision making and the assigning of responsibility for carrying out the action. This phase of the design worked least well. Some of the problems could have been avoided.

After lunch on Sunday, the total group met to share plans from the morning discussions and to deal with any last minute business before the workshop ended. A number of action proposals were made. These included items like:

a school council of parents and teachers meeting monthly;

the organization of social evenings after the workshop;

a committee to coordinate the writing of a report on the workshop; this report to be sent to the Department of Education, other schools, and other interested parties;

several more open meetings to be held at the various schools so that parents and teachers can get together to meet each other and to discuss school problems.

After these proposals had been reported, we tried to pin down exactly who was going to take responsibility for each one. Here we ran into some difficulty. No one seemed willing to really commit himself to making sure the various projects actually happened. This seems to have been the result of at least two factors.

First, at this last meeting a member of the general community at large had been invited by the staff to be present. This person had been active in helping to set up the workshop and had some potential for helping to implement further action. However, he was seen as an unknown quantity by some of the participants, even though his appearance at this last session had been announced early in the workshop.

Second, many of the participants wanted to check back with their friends, superiors and other groups back home before committing themselves to any long-range action plans.

After about an hour's discussion, it was decided to plan only two firm action steps at that point. The first of these was to form a subcommittee to design a data collection form to assess the immediate feelings about the workshop and its outcomes. This committee would collect the data, get it copied for anyone interested, and distribute it to all participants and other interested parties. The second action step was to decide to meet two weeks after the workshop to decide whether further action should be taken. In the meantime, all participants were to check with friends, superiors, and others to determine what problems they thought should be worked on and if they were interested in joining the workshop group. This last decision was clearly an attempt to keep the action possibilities alive. As a result of the meeting after the workshop, the actions reported earlier in this paper took place.

Groupings used. The design used a variety of groupings. These included working as a total group, in homogeneous groups of teachers or parents, and in smaller cross groups composed of both teachers and parents. With the exception of the total group, membership in each of the groups changed continuously throughout the workshop. This was intentional since we wanted to build a total community and to avoid cliques as much as possible.

Generally, the mix of groupings worked out well. Only two real problems arose from the groupings used and these were predictable. First, the total group was too large for free discussion. Some of the participants had trouble getting 'air time' and others found it easy to withdraw. Second, in the homogeneous groups, there was a tendency to retreat into accepted positions and comfortable clichés rather than to deal with the issues.

Relations within Subgroups

As the workshop developed, it became clear that there were a number of issues which needed to be dealt with within each subgroup. Issues between teachers from different schools were sometimes apparent and occasionally got in the way of the total group. Our argument is not that we should ensure that there is no difference of opinion within each subgroup, but rather that these differences need to be considered when selecting participants. If the differences of opinion within each subgroup are too large, it is difficult to generate the climate of trust and respect required to explore the larger issues. During the workshop we described here, this slowed down the discussion of some issues, e.g. Black Power and school discipline. On the other hand, the openly expressed differences within each group often helped in breaking down intergroup barriers.

Power and Influence Structure

Another important and controversial issue raised was whether the workshop was likely to change the power balance between the parties involved or to merely make people more comfortable with the existing (uneven) distribution of power and influence in the community. About all we could say beforehand, was that we were not sure. Power redistribution was not one of our goals for the workshop, but in working toward action to be carried out after the workshop, we thought it might be necessary to deal with the power issue.

In actuality, the power issue did not seem to be as major an issue as we had anticipated. Black Power was mentioned a few times but never really discussed. Power battles never developed. This may have been due to the fact that the most power-concerned parents had chosen not to participate in the workshop. Whether or not the workshop could have survived a major power conflict is still unclear.

Although the actual power balance was never really challenged during the workshop, there was a genuine interest in increasing the influence of the individuals and the group. This was true of both parents and teachers. But, for these participants, influence was to be based on cooperation and trust in other groups (including those in power). This cooperation and trust between the groups involved seem to have increased as a result of the workshop.

The model we described at the beginning was useful to us in trying to understand this workshop. The issues raised by the workshop in terms of training technology have also helped to clarify for us some of the areas where more study is needed. Unfortunately, it is beyond the scope of this paper to deal with all of them. A larger report on the research attached to this project is in preparation. This preliminary report is presented in the hope that other people who are also searching for better methods of solving multiracial and community problems will be able to build on our experience.

References

1   *Culver, C.M.; Dunham, F.; Edgerton, J.W., and Edgerton, M.:* Community service workers and recipients: a combined middle class/lower class workshop. J. appl. behav. Sci. *5:* 519–535 (1969).
2   *Klein, E.B.; Thomas, C.S., and Bellis, E.:* When warring groups meet: the use of a group approach in police/black community relations. Soc. Psychiat. *6:* 93–99 (1971).

3   *Levin, G. and Stein, D.D.:* System intervention in a school-community conflict. J. appl. behav. Sci. *6:* 337–352 (1970).
4   *Rubin, I.:* The reduction of prejudice through laboratory training. J. appl. behav. Sci. *3:* 29–50 (1967).
5   *Walton, R.E.:* A problem-solving workshop on border conflicts in Eastern Africa. J. appl. behav. Sci. *6:* 453–489 (1970).

Authors' address: Dr. *Kurt E. Olmosk* and Mr. *Gert Graversen*, Organization Development Unit, Department of Management Studies, University of Leeds, *Leeds 6* (England)

Interpers. Develop. *3:* 115–139 (1972)

Group Training as an Aid to Staff Development in Psychiatric Institutions

R. Sandison

Southampton Mental Health Centre, Southampton

The effects of the mental hospital on its patients and on its staff have been well documented in a number of studies. *Stanton and Schwarz* (16), *Jones and Sidebotham* (8), *Bickford et al.* (2), *Wing and Brown* (18) may be quoted as examples. Little is known, however, about the communication problems of hospitals examined in the light of insights into communication processes derived from T-group experiences.

A recent broadcast drama concerned a group of people who went to a house as guests and who then found, for various reasons, that they were unable to leave. This is no new situation to mental hospitals, where the 'guests' after months or years in the institution, lack all desire to depart. *Martin* (9), pointed out that the state of institutionalization occurs in a patient 'who has ceased to question his position as a patient, and who has become too passive to present any problems of management, but in the process of necessity has lost much of his individuality and initiative.' The condition is not confined to any diagnostic group, occurring in depressives, neurotics and alcoholics, as well as psychotics. He thought the condition was chronic and contributed to by doctors and nurses who had come wholly or partly under the control of the system.

My own experience with therapy groups and T-groups led me to look at the psychiatric institution at which I worked, with the insights derived from my knowledge of small and large group processes. During the past three years, I have established staff groups and seminars run wholly or partly on T-group lines. From this study, I have been able to come to some conclusions about staff groups and staff-patient groups and about the effects of T-group training on communication within the hospital.

During these three years, the institution itself was changing for other reasons. The most important of these have been the structure for nursing administration and the 'cog-wheel' system of medical administration. Lay administration has remained relatively unchanged, but has been considerably influenced by the changes in the other disciplines.

The Psychiatric Unit

Before it is possible to understand the kind of impact which staff T-groups may be expected to have on psychiatric units, it will be helpful to look at their communication systems and their culture. In commencing this study, one might first look at the numbers of levels of communication. It is generally agreed that industrial organizations having between 100 and 999 employees attract three or more levels of supervision. Mental hospitals of average size employ a total of staff falling within this range and their evolution in the hundred years from 1860 to 1960 followed this pattern quite faithfully. Nurses had levels of supervision at ward sister, assistant matron and matron, the latter being responsible to the medical superintendent, who was the statutory chief officer of the hospital until 1959. Most of the departments had only two levels of supervision and the senior doctors enjoyed only one, the medical superintendent. The medical superintendent was responsible to a committee, itself answerable to the county or borough council, but these bodies were capable of a good deal of manipulation by an astute superintendent. Such a system had much to commend it, provided that the powerful office of superintendent was filled by a liberal and forward-looking doctor. In some cases, however, small-minded men of tyrannical disposition ruled their village states, with consequences which have been documented more frequently by patients than staff. This is not entirely surprising, since successful applicants for the posts of medical superintendent in the 1920s and 1930s were usually those who could produce evidence that they could run the hospital more cheaply than the other candidates. Naturally, county and borough councils wanted no scandals at their mental hospitals, and from their point of view, the more institutionalized the patients were, the less trouble there was likely to be.

The changes which have occurred in psychiatric hospitals since the Mental Health Act of 1959 have been complex and are perhaps too recent to allow us to form a clear overall picture. On the one hand, there has been a move towards democracy, largely dictated from the Ministry of Health (now the Department of Health). Medical superintendents have all but disappeared, replaced by the so-called 'cog-wheel' system of medical committees. Hospitals have been divided by the establishment of teams, and consultants have final clinical responsibility. Numbers of inpatients have fallen, whilst day hospitals have proliferated. On the other hand, there has been a strong move towards each profession creating a complex hierarchy of its own. Possibly the most complex has been the Salmon nursing structure, which creates no less than five levels of supervision at grades 6, 7, 8, 9 and 10. This has been closely followed by local authority social workers who appear, to the practising psychiatrist, to have almost all become supervisors, leaving few workers in the field of mental health. Already, in some hospitals, where there is no nurse training school, the patients are liable to be nursed by agency nurses, many of whom are untrained. Psychiatric social workers have largely deserted psychiatric institutions to work in social services departments, child psychiatry, or universities. Doctors, rather less than nurses, have also proliferated their levels of supervision. Under local authority management, assistant medical officer, senior or deputy, and superintendent were the only grades. Now we have senior house officers, registrars, senior registrars, assistant psychiatrists and consultants, not to speak of the addition, in academic units, of lecturers, senior lecturers and a professor. Such an array must sadly bewilder nursing staff, accustomed until not so long ago to the 'ward doctor'.

Although we cannot be certain what is happening to and in psychiatric institutions, some new phenomena are occurring. One of these concerns revelations made by nursing staff, often students, into malpractices and repressive activities to the authorities or the public. *Robb* (12) in 'Sans Everything' made accusations, many of which were refuted in a subsequent enquiry, against Friern Barnet Hospital. The allegations of cruelty to patients at Farleigh Hospital in the past three years have attracted widespread publicity and concern, whilst allegations of exploitation of patients were recently made against the staff of Whittington Hospital by student nurses (17). This phenomenon is no doubt just one of the torches being carried by students all over the world in the 1970s and is likely to remain a force with which hospital authorities will have to reckon. The medical superintendent under whom I trained would sometimes say at meetings of the medical staff; 'If we do not fight for the patient, no-one else will.' Today, 25 years on, it may be that the student nurse is the only one left to fight for him.

Patients in Hospital

So that we can retain perspective in this brief survey of recent changes in mental hospitals, it might be helpful to look at what patients have had to say. Going back as far as 1900, their preoccupations over the years have largely been with such matters as fear of certification, fears of reprisals from the staff, frustration at the failure of the staff to understand and communicate with patients. *Beers* (1), as long ago as 1908, spoke not only of his single-handed battle with his own psychosis, but also of a long drawn-out struggle with the violence and insensitivity of the staff, resulting in episodes in which at least one of the other patients died. *Hales* (6) was concerned with mistaken diagnosis and wrongful certification, while *Dawson* (3), in a novel, sensitively worked out some of the ways in which patients can help each other. At the same time, she refers to the feeling of remoteness and strangeness of interviews with her psychiatrist.

A different approach was described by *Winterton,* a journalist who became a patient in a mental hospital in order to study the hospital system from the inside. In a very fair appraisal of the average county mental hospital of that period he says: 'To be afflicted by insanity is probably the most overwhelming of human disasters. Perhaps for that very reason, most people take it for granted that they will never be directly affected by it and do their best to forget it exists.' Making a plea that unlawful detention rarely if ever occurred, the author nevertheless records that 'at Rainhill Hospital, in 1936, 133 patients had been, during a period of nine months, secluded for a total of 12,049 hours', which was a considerable reduction compared with the previous year.

Finally, in this series, *Simpson* (15) wrote a book in which she describes all the most negative feelings which a young woman could possibly have about mental hospitals. A change of hospital, a sympathetic doctor, a hopeful attitude on the part of the nursing staff, enabled her to readjust. Significantly, she started to get well when the psychiatrist no longer went to see her in the ward, but she went to him.

Staff about Staff

In recent years, reports by patients have been published less often and there are no doubt reasons for this. It may be that there is a connection between this decline and the increase in the numbers of studies by the psychiatric staff about staff. *John* (1), in 'The Study of the Psychiatric Nurse', draws attention to the problems of role finding and communication with her patients which trouble the nurse. *McGhee* (10), in 'The Patient's Attitude to Nursing Care', has done something similar with general hospital nurses. *Rognow* (13), in 'The Psychiatrists' directs attention to important relationships between mental hospitals in the USA and their staffs. That a professor of political science should study psychiatrists is a new phenomenon, that he should say, 'If the admittedly small sample of public mental hospital psychiatrists is any guide, it would appear that the psychiatrists in such institutions not only practise a different psychiatry from their colleagues in private practice but that they are different people as well', would appear to be an indictment of the mental hospital system. Other behavioural scientists continue to perpetuate myths about patients which must tend to keep the mental hospital in business. *Ryder and Silver* (14), in 'Modern English Society', put the sociologists' point of view. 'According to many sociologists today who reject the medical illness analogy, mental illness is just as much a form of deviance as are the more obvious forms of crime and delinquency. Moreover, it often grows out of the same conditions. ... Not surprisingly, then, crime and delinquency again show characteristic social patterns – in relation to both the kinds of offences committed and the forms of treatment (or punishment) imposed.' That the patient really has little to say is suggested by *Fromm* (5) in 'Fear of Freedom'. The position of many patients vis-à-vis psychiatry and its institutions is summed up by *Fromm:* 'The neurotic person is the one who has not given up fighting against complete submission, but who, at the same time, has remained bound to the figure of the magic helper, whatever form or shape he may have assumed. His neurosis is always to be understood as an attempt, and essentially an unsuccessful one, to solve the conflict between that basic dependency and the quest for freedom.'

Even when patients have been invited to say something about their own hospitals, the study tends to be designed in such a way as to prevent the patient from saying anything valid. The most recent of very few studies is by *Raphael and Peers* (11), 'Psychiatric Hospitals Viewed by their Patients'. Despite its attractive title it is impossible to glean anything from this report as to what psychiatric patients *really* feel about their situation and the report makes assumptions, such as the assumption that locked wards are necessary, which suggests that there is little expectation of radical change in the culture of the average hospital.

Since patients are bound between society's view of them and their own dependence, they would appear, therefore, to have little power in the psychiatric setting. Psychiatrists have had curiously little to say in the past 15 years which is in any way progressive, and they remain in guilty silence over the state of their hospitals and indeed often seem unaware of what is going on. Administrators might be seen by the cynic to be unconcerned as to whether their institution deals in sick people or not, while nurses are making themselves heard from their officially lowest grade, i.e. the students. We would do well to ponder that it is the Department of Health in their report 'Hospital Services for the Mentally Ill' which has proposed that mental hospitals should close in 15 years. Alas for such faith! Already the psychiatrists are in a state of disbelief, *Freeman* (4) going so far as to say: 'However, when it gets on to the closure of mental hospitals, it reaches the realms of archetypal fantasy.' Already, it is said that some of the new psychiatric units in general hospitals are asking for new buildings to house long-stay patients. Mental hospitals will tend to remain because most psychiatrists and administrators want them to remain, to fulfil their own needs, while nurses are overcome with the myth that their closure will throw them out of a job. With the likelihood, therefore, that large psychiatric institutions will be with us for many years, we may now consider some of the patient/staff and staff/staff relationships which can be observed.

The staff themselves, during frequent phases of frustration, complain mostly of lack of communication, failure in consultation, and of decisions appearing to be made by faceless members of staff who cannot be identified. *Jones and Sidebotham* (8) recall the nurse tutor who decided to put his pathetic sum of £ 75 allowed for the annual purchase of equipment towards a tape recorder. This proposal was turned down: 'He is not sure by whom, or at what level.'

It is tempting to see what is happening as a bid for power and status by those whose disciplines were relatively impotent under the superintendent or house governor system. More likely it is a complex phenomenon designed to create status without anxiety. What happens in practice is that those of higher status become removed from direct contact with patients and frequently even from those who are in contact with the patients. This avoidance of contact with the actual product is a distinct possibility in industry, where those on the factory floor have the lowest status and where the directors need never have seen the factory product. In industry, however, one seldom graduates from factory floor to director, as in the health service, and entry to managerial posts is through a different portal to, say, the artisans and fitters. However, now that graduates are entering hospital administration and there are graduate courses for nurses, the National Health Service may become more like industry in its modes of entry to different grades.

I have so far suggested that there is something about institutional dynamics which in the case of hospitals produces staff frustration, stifles communication and creates in the patients either states of hostility or of passive acceptance. The report of the enquiry into Whittingham Hospital states: 'We are left with the general impression of a hospital whose nurses have had all too little encouragement and opportunity to break away from the predominantly custodial role which is now little more than a blur in the memory of their colleagues in many psychiatric hospitals elsewhere.' These are comforting words to those who do not happen to work at Whittingham, but the truth is more likely to be that the majority of the patients in most of our mental hospitals are thoroughly institutionalized, though in general living in humane conditions and looked after by a kindly and indulgent staff. In my own hospital, one ward sister of a typical long-stay ward is proud of the fact that no patient who comes into her office ever left without being given a biscuit or piece of chocolate.

What, therefore, does happen in the average 'good' mental hospital, where the staff are mostly convinced that a Whittingham situation 'could never happen here'. Certain patterns of happening tend to repeat themselves and may, therefore, be classified as syndromes.

The Syndrome of 'Being a Patient'

Traditionally, in every kind of hospital, patients have to be controlled, depersonalised and processed in distinct ways. Patients are severely censured for making suggestions about their own treatment, for manipulating their own medication, for discharging themselves or for refusing operations. The highly trained staff know what is best for them and, just in case the patient is likely to object, certain brain-washing procedures are standard. For example, in general hospitals he is kept in bed, wears an identification wristlet and communication with the outside world is severely restricted and the day is divided by a strict routine. It is of interest that homely comforts and outside contacts such as newspapers, books and sweets and fruit are provided by private enterprise and voluntary organizations. Radio and television are frequently the gift of organizations like 'Friends of the Hospital'. Although these measures and procedures have a rational explanation, their objective clearly seems to be to minimise contact between patient and staff and to keep the patient in a state of subjection. One of the features of restrictive hospital practices such as restriction on the visiting of sick children, is that the hospital doggedly resists change and that the measures greatly exceed those required to control patients. Anyone who visits an outpatient department or who goes to a general practitioner's surgery will be aware of the state of depersonalisation and submission induced by the contact with authority alone.

In mental hospitals, the position the patient finds himself in is much worse. Historically, the fear of mental illness was an important factor, hence asylums were in the country, wards were locked and patients were totally segregated.

There are many signs that such controls are the least frightening way of dealing with mental illness. About 20 years ago, I found myself working in a hospital which up until then had been run on strictly custodial lines. Great numbers of the chronically ill patients had had all their teeth removed on the grounds that oral sepsis was a cause of insanity. On one of my first visits to a ward called the 'female refractory ward', I found that nearly all the patients were on bread and milk diets which they scooped out of bowls with their fingers. When I suggested that these patients should all go on normal diet I was told by the ward sister that this would make the patients too strong and that she and her staff would be overpowered by them. Control by straight jacket has gone, and control by locked room and locked ward is going, although still with us. Control by drugs and ECT, is, however, practised almost universally on psychiatric patients, the rationalisation for this being that the patient is 'ill' and requires 'treatment'. The two great fears of mental hospital staffs are of sexual activity between the patients and that they will run away. The former means that countless long-stay patients, most of whom are nowadays well over 50 years of age, spend most of their lives segregated from the opposite sex, whilst the latter perpetuates the idea that mental hospital patients are dangerous, that they are liable to 'escape' and that they must at all costs be brought back. Within my personal experience, I know many such patients who eventually made good their 'escape' from the hospital and who subsequently managed to live remarkably normal lives in the community. Some of these patients were, when I first knew them, spending most of their time in solitary confinement as a result of attempts to leave the hospital, and often acted out situations such as breaking windows and threatening suicide. On each occasion, at different hospitals, that I have been involved in the setting-up of patient communities where the patients were taught to accept responsibility for their own recovery, there have been considerable difficulties. There have been rumours of sexual licence on the unit, and complaints of lack of precision in treatment programmes and of patients' behaviour outside the hospital. If one sticks it out, even after initial setbacks, the institution and community accept the situation after a time.

There are a number of other syndromes which arise out of the 'being-a-patient' syndrome.

The 'Maximum-Security-Ward' Syndrome

In one hospital where I worked, we evolved to the happy position where no wards were locked and in which no ward could be identified as being 'disturbed' or 'refractory'. The year was 1956 and largactil was beginning to be used in a number of the patients which, although a control in itself, helped the staff to accept disturbance more readily. A visiting American psychiatrist arrived one day and demanded to be taken to the 'maximum security ward'. On being told that there was no such ward he expressed disbelief, so I took him to the mens' ward where rather more of the disturbed patients lived. As we passed through the unlocked door, he told me that in a similar American state hospital there would be double locked doors with two nurses at the door, that the ward would be devoid of curtains, tablecloths or other civilised comforts and that within the ward would be a wire cage in which recalcitrant patients would be placed. It occurred to me on remembering this anecdote that mental hospitals have a need, as part of their unconscious dynamic structure, to keep the concept of the locked ward and of the dangerous patient. Over 25 years of working with psychiatric patients have convinced me that patients are invariably frightened, persecuted, unhappy or anxious, and that any violence is only that of the cornered animal. It seems that the locked, disturbed or refractory ward is the place where the hospital can concentrate its hostility towards patients and its need for control, perhaps allowing the exercise of greater freedom elsewhere.

The 'She's-Eaten-it' Syndrome

This syndrome is seen in long-stay wards where patient disturbance has been controlled by psychotropic drugs, often changed with great diligence and ingenuity by the medical staff and often combined into elegant prescriptions. In 1971, I was, for about six months, in medical charge of such a ward, where I introduced staff seminars on T-group lines, the effects of which will be referred to later. The ward contained 35 female patients of the most deteriorated kind, most of whom had been labelled as schizophrenic, mentally subnormal or epileptic, or combinations of these. Only three patients had any regular contact with relatives and only nine patients regularly left the ward to work in industrial or occupational therapy. At the start, there was no opportunity for occupying the patients in the ward, they were able to go into a concrete and grass courtyard in fine weather where they mostly sat on benches or walked around. The ward is of the corridor type with many single rooms, a design favoured by *John Conolly* a hundred years ago. Most of the patients had been in the ward for a great many years. One, aged 83 years, had been in the hospital since the age of six. When I found myself in charge of these patients, I went to the ward and started to tell the ward sister that all I intended to do for the first week or two was to observe what went on and that I would change nothing until the staff and I had got to know each other and had worked together as a group. Whilst I was talking with the sister, a nurse rushed in carrying some underclothing, saying, 'She's eaten it.' This, I discovered, was to impress upon me what a difficult, frustrating and unrewarding task they had with many of the patients. The one about whom she was talking ate compulsively everything that looked edible. She would eat plants, the leaves off the trees, string, rope, clothing. I found that her dress was always put on back to front to stop her eating the buttons off it. The nurses in this ward were kindly and understanding, but the only way they knew of dealing with behaviour disturbance was to report it to the doctor who would 'control' it by yet more drugs or another ingenious combination of drugs. This was rendered easier as the drug firms obligingly produced new drugs every few weeks or months. I was the new doctor, who would be sure to know some yet more powerful drug which would reduce or stop the patient's deviant behaviour. They felt at first confused and let down when all I had to offer was that I wanted to observe and talk with people.

The 'Mental-Illness' Syndrome

Much has been written in recent years about the question of which model will most appropriately convey the concept most usually known as mental illness, but formerly known as insanity, lunacy, madness, witchcraft or possession. Doctors have been greatly concerned with the mentally ill since the 18th century and since that date have formulated ideas which constitute the greater part of the psychiatric textbooks of today. Thus, the standard works on psychiatry are derived from observations made on a rather special group of people, those whose disordered minds combined with social and family circumstances to result in their going to mental hospitals. Authors such as *Foulds, Sczacz, Laing and Smythies* have pointed out that there are a number of alternative models to the medical one and that several if not all of these more appropriately describe the kinds of people seen by psychiatrists outside mental hospitals.

The great pioneers of psychotherapy started from medically dominated environments, *Freud* in neurology and *Jung* in the Burghölzli mental hospital. The early writings of both men are heavily influenced by these environments. *Freud*'s early studies were with hysterics mimicking neurological disease whilst some of *Jung*'s were with schizophrenia. Both nevertheless freed themselves from the shackles of medical symptomatology and studied the people who had the symptoms thereby giving psychiatry its proper objective. We thus have at present a position developing in which social workers, community-orientated nurses, members of helping organizations and psychotherapists see those who come for their help primarily as people, whilst most of the staff in psychiatric hospitals see them as patients with symptoms. I put no value judgement on this. Although my own attitude is well biased towards a psychotherapeutic and community-orientated approach, it is perfectly possible to justify the strictly medical approach, provided one is consistent. The wind of change, however, blows more strongly away from the mental hospital with its phenomenological approach, and its direction is maintained by a new generation of social workers, doctors and nurses. Yet the training of psychiatrists and psychiatric nurses still remains institutionally-orientated and much may have to be unlearnt at a later date.

The principle victim is the patient. The young woman who does not eat is, whilst in hospital, a 'case of anoxia nervosa', when she leaves and goes, say to a day hospital, she may be confused to find that her symptom is ignored and emphasis placed on family or sexual relationships. In hospital, the depressive gets ECT, in another setting he may find himself in a therapeutic group discussing his life problems. No wonder patients in psychosis units produce psychotic symptoms, which change to neurotic ones when they are transferred to neurosis units! The same patient will emphasise phobic symptoms when with the psychiatrist, but with the social worker he will emphasise his marital problems. How is the patient to know whether his habit, say of having to stop his car periodically to check whether he has knocked a cyclist down is an obsessive compulsive symptom, or a result of extreme anxiety about his sexual potency. As *Jung* once observed, 40 years ago, there is no such thing as a confused patient, only confused doctors. It might be as well at this point to state some objectives which might result in this confusion to patients being reduced. We should then see what mental hospitals have done already to meet these objectives and what contribution the T-group style of insights can make to furthering them.

Objectives in Psychiatry

(1) More careful assessments of the patient, his environment and his needs, both in the community and in hospital.

(2) The breaking down of interdisciplinary barriers and the formation of effective multidisciplinary teams.

(3) Involvement of staff at all levels in the therapeutic process.

(4) The raising of patient status and preservation of the human dignity of the patient. The patient to assume greater responsibility in his own treatment. The barriers between 'patient' and 'non-patient' within the same family should be reduced, as should distinctions between staff and patients.

(5) Inpatient units should become more therapeutically and less medically orientated.

(6) Training should be provided in group techniques for all staff in contact with patients.

In the past, some hospitals, mostly through individual pioneers such as *Bell, Rees and Maxwell Jones,* have recognised these objectives and have taken steps to achieve them. The open door system of the 1940s and the therapeutic communities of the 1950s are examples. Many of the techniques used by T.P. *Rees* are models today for institutional psychiatrists, others can be criticised on the grounds that they defeated their own objectives. *Rees* treated his psychotics as people, and achieved, in the 1940s the feat of reducing his compulsory admissions to about 4 %. A seriously disturbed psychotic patient who refused admission would be brought to the hospital and shown round as if he were a visiting professor. When a member of his own management committee developed acute mania, he admitted him to one of his wards and as soon as he was convalescent, insisted that he attend committee meetings. Shortly before *Rees* died, I visited him in his private consulting rooms in London, where the room was dominated by a magnificent couch. 'My next patient is a schizophrenic', he confided, 'He can't stand it in here – we'll go out round the corner and have a glass of beer and a sandwich together.'

The therapeutic community seeks to create an atmosphere in which all contribute to therapy including of course the patients. In mental hospitals, its desiderata include such things as the need to integrate male and female wards, to give more power and freedom to patients, and to create a system whereby the whole community can analyse and understand its own behaviour. Of course, some units have further to go than others to become therapeutic. It is only about five years since I discovered a box in a so-called neurosis unit which contained money from patients who had been fined for talking about their problems to each other. The principle fears of the staff are centred around sexual licence (on the part of the patients), whether the patients will escape and whether they will become too strong.

The therapeutic community, properly executed, goes far towards solving a number of problems for both patients and staff. The patients have a forum for expressing their feelings, the staff are largely protected from one to one encounters, anxiety over sexual expression is diminished because it is discussed by the whole group. The staff usually become strongly identified with the objectives of the community and can thus withstand external criticism. I hasten to add that few mental hospitals actually operate therapeutic communities although many claim to do so.

As mental hospitals are, therefore, resistant to therapeutic communities and there may well be disadvantages in such a system anyway, what alternatives are there if our objectives are to be realised? The solution, or its beginnings, can only be realised through the staff. It is not money but attitudes which will determine how the psychiatric patient is treated and I now propose to describe what has been done in the Southampton area in the past three years to aid personal development of psychiatric staff.

The Origins of T-Group Training for Psychiatric Staff

Group therapy and group activities have taken place in various forms in psychiatric institutions for many years. Therapy groups were in being in a few hospitals, mostly in the London area, in the 1940s. The success of deep insulin treatment for schizophrenia largely lay in the patients being treated together as a group, spending nearly all their time with a small group of nurses. Patients in mental hospitals commonly work as groups in such departments as art and occupational therapy. The extent to which they are encouraged to communicate in such departments varies. It is still not unknown for patients to have to work in occupational therapy in complete silence. Probably in most departments the main objective is the work itself, in a few the work is designed to help the patient communicate his problems at a group level. Since art therapists and occupational therapists normally have no formal training in group methods, their departments tend to lack therapeutic effectiveness.

In some wards of psychiatric hospitals, the student nurses are still discouraged from talking with the patients or from engaging in group activities with them. Where attitudes are changing, the nursing staff may be found with small groups of patients and it is not uncommon, at least in admission wards, for patients to get together in small spontaneously formed groups in which, inevitably, their problems are shared out. Most patients, nevertheless, in admission units, express the belief that their problems should be and normally only are discussed with a doctor.

There are thus many arguments to justify the formation of staff/patient therapy groups in the wards of mental hospitals. To recapitulate, many activities already occur in groups and, when allowed to do so, patients tend to form groups of their own. Additional reasons are that small group therapy forms a valuable learning experience for the patient, obtainable in no other way. He learns, for example, the meaning of identification and commitment to a group, he learns to share his problems with people other than doctors, he learns something about trust, and, by measuring his problem against the problems of others, he can put it in perspective.

Just as there are good reasons for developing staff/patient groups, there are equally valid and interrelated reasons for setting up staff groups. The long preamble to this chapter which described some of the conditions in mental hospitals and some common staff tensions and staff attitudes largely arises because staff seldom communicate with one another at a personal level. Unless staff are close personal friends they seldom know much about each other. The hierarchical structure makes it difficult for different grades of staff to communicate and it is indeed possible for a student nurse to go through her training without having spoken to a consultant. In long-stay wards, the nursing staff may have little idea as to the outlook and policy of the consultant and indeed may have little contact with him. In admission wards, consultants may deal almost exclusively with the senior nursing staff, with the result that the student nurses have little idea as to what is happening, medically speaking, to the patients.

We might at this point summarise the desiderata for making a psychiatric unit a more effective therapeutic instrument.

(1) To create a ward environment in which group therapeutic techniques are accepted by the staff. In most wards, group therapy has low priority and the group leaders are constantly frustrated by finding that their patients are elsewhere at the appointed time.

(2) To provide training for all members of staff which will alter their attitudes in the direction of greater sensitivity towards the needs of their patients.

(3) To organise the staff into a team, with common objectives in terms of patient care, who are sensitive towards each other's personalities and needs. The staff group's aims will be towards identification with and committment to unit policy which each member has had a hand in shaping.

(4) To support one another in staff relationships towards the institution as a whole. Institutional life is full of frustrations and the development of negative feelings towards the administration distorts judgement and paralyses effort. The unit, if it is to be really effective, must devise ways of managing its relationship to the administration and higher authority.

Before discussing ways in which T-group methods can meet these desiderata, we may consider whether these objectives are healthy for the patients as well as the staff. There are several studies which show that staff tensions in individuals affect patient behaviour and that conflict or hostility between members of the staff adversely affects patients and retards progress. We must also take note of what a patient of mine has called 'staff/patient warfare' about which much less has been written. Unquestionably it goes on in all hospitals and psychiatric units, unhappily also in those which regard themselves as therapeutic communities. If the insights gained from T-groups are to do anything, therefore, they should help to resolve the staff/patient warfare problem.

Evolving Culture of Group Work Course

In 1968, on the initiative of *Ruth Heller,* a group of tutors in Southampton decided to start a T-group course for social workers in the area. Much of how the course developed is described elsewhere in this book, but the constitution of the original staff group must be seen to have a great deal of bearing on what subsequently happened. There were two psychiatric social workers, one of whom had a small service commitment to the psychiatric hospital, there were two psychiatrists, both associated closely with the same hospital, there was a lecturer in the extramural department, a lecturer in the psychology department and there was a psychiatric social worker from the child psychiatry service and a member of the probation service. The fact that in 1972 all but two of the original members of the team of eight are still working together to run T-group courses is itself an indication that the multidisciplinary team approach is central to the philosophy of the Southampton group work courses. This was immediately reflected in the membership of the courses which rapidly diversified to include doctors, nurses, clergy, teachers, prison officers and other members of helping professions. Unique, we believe, to the Southampton courses, have been the 20 or more follow-up meetings after the intensive week's course, thus promoting the objective of a group of people working for a longish time together to achieve common aims.

It has thus come about that over the years a number of staff at the psychiatric hospital and its associated day centre have been through the group work course. The practical results of this will now be briefly summarised before we go on to describe the impact of staff T-groups on the organization.

The most obvious practical result has been the establishment of a number of therapy groups. These are associated with the admission wards, with the day hospital and with the outpatient psychiatric services. In all these groups, the leadership is paired, thus following the trainer pattern (in the Southampton group work course.) As more people are trained it has become possible to make a rule that no one shall run a group unless he has attended the group work course. This need not apply to both therapy group leaders, the second member being usually less experienced and, therefore, in a training role. The leadership pair are normally of opposite sexes and of different disciplines. Thus we have groups in which doctor and nurse, nurse and social worker, doctor and social work trainee, doctor and occupational therapist constitute the leadership pair, to give a few examples.

As the groups grew in number, it became evident that the leaders, few of whom were greatly experienced, required some kind of support. This has been met partly by an annual 'advanced' course held at Southampton University by the extramural department, open to all those who, having attended the basic course, were running groups. There was an additional need for a more ongoing kind of support, as the advanced course is limited to ten weekly sessions in the autumn term. The author is, therefore, conducting a fortnightly seminar for all those running groups in the *psychiatric* service in the area. Clearly, there is an unmet need for similar facilities to provide support for those in other organizations in the area who are running groups. This seminar deals with problems within the groups mostly, but occasionally leaders will draw attention to administrative difficulties, usually those working in inpatient units.

The Southampton model of T-group training has now developed certain cultural characteristics which are being reflected by the developing culture of the psychiatric units in the area. Central to these cultural characteristics is the existence of a multidisciplinary team of trainers who have worked together for several years. One member, however, is no longer working with the team for reasons to do with attitudes and leadership style, a happening which has been reflected in at least one of the service units. The course itself is work-orientated, the members of the groups knowing that whatever happens on the intensive week's course, they have to meet together again for 20 weeks following. There is also an expectation that members of the course will themselves run groups in the area and there is as much emphasis on staff groups and inter-staff relationships as on therapy and other staff/client types of groups.

Formation of Staff T-Groups

From the foregoing it is to be expected that the group work courses would lead to the formation of staff T-groups and four of these have been started, not including a T-group-style weekly staff meeting which ran for about three months in one of the long-stay wards. One of these four staff T-groups was started by the author in an admission ward and this is now being successfully continued under the leadership of a colleague well experienced in group techniques. The second group was started in another admission unit by a graduate of the group work course, but was subsequently abandoned. The third was at the day hospital and was set up by another doctor who had attended the course. When I joined the staff of the day hospital in October, 1971, I joined this group. Its subsequent history is given in more detail below. The fourth group was started independently of the group work course at the adolescent unit by a doctor who is an analyst. Some of the members of his team have attended the course, and run their own groups.

Some points about these staff T-groups will already have suggested themselves. There is a single 'leader', he is invariably a doctor and he is the senior doctor in the unit. This would appear to have been an inevitable rather than an evolutionary occurrence. The senior doctor, usually a consultant, will be seen by the staff as the leader in other day-to-day situations and any other choice might seem contrived. Many problems, however, confront the leader who is also the leader of the team. For example, how far is leadership role compatible with his being a member of the group? To what extent can he reach and expose his own conflicts and problems without eroding his own role? Will the group ever feel safe enough to reveal feelings honestly while the boss is there so to speak? It has been suggested that a possible way out of this dilemma would be for the experienced members in the area to 'take' each others groups, but there are practical and cultural objections to this. The Southampton group work course tutors, faced with the problem, invite once a year a colleague from the University of Sussex, to head a one-day T-group for its members. Once again, following the cultural pattern of the parent body, the day hospital (mental health centre) team invited him to lead a two-day T-group 'course' which had some clear-cut objectives and which profoundly affected the whole course of the Centre's development.

Other practical difficulties had to be worked through. If all the staff of the unit were to be included, the group would be too large, and there would be no one left to look after the patients. Some members of the team might not wish to join. Was membership of the group to be denied to temporary members of the team, such as student nurses? Many of these problems were discussed at length and worked through in the admission ward where I started my first staff T-group. The prototype of this group had been a rather large group of staff who met once a week after the community meeting of all staff and patients. At this staff meeting, the content of the community meeting was discussed, and it therefore seemed natural to start talking about ourselves and our own tensions. For a long time, we were hung up on whether to use Christian names or to abandon nurses' and occupational therapists' uniforms. There was great reluctance to give up old safe attitudes and methods of behaviour. It was not until the following year, when two further members of the team had attended the course that suddenly, it seemed, the barriers of title and uniform collapsed. The staff decided, guiltily, to form a T-group consisting of the permanent members of the nursing, medical, social work and occupational therapy disciplines who were working on the unit. This left the ward maids and student nurses and the night nurses. These had, not always regularly, attended the previous, larger, prototype group, so we felt that we had lost something. In order to resolve the problem we had thus created of setting up a rather smug T-group of senior staff, I started another group, a sort of all-comers group, which also met once a week. This was mostly attended by the student nurses, although a doctor and a social worker were regular attenders: the ward maids and the night nurses never came and their absence was perhaps the reason for continued lack of communication between day and night staff which led frequently to confused handling of the patients.

A difficulty inherent to inpatient staff T-groups arose out of the nurses' shift system. This meant that only a proportion of nurses were 'on duty' at any one time and although occasionally nurses would come in who were off duty, the shift system imposes severe limitations on staff T-groups in inpatient units. Despite this, there was a very good feeling of commitment to the group and most staff felt that it took precedence over all other activities except emergencies.

What was learnt from this staff T-group? We learnt from this inpatient staff T-group that such a concept was perfectly feasible and did not, in that instance, lead to disruption of the group or major clashes with the administration outside the unit. The group became much more effective as soon as members other than the leader had attended the group work course. It certainly led to the breaking down of interdisciplinary barriers and the formation of a more effective team. For example, the social workers, occupational therapist and art therapist became much more part of the clinical team. The social workers found themselves making more positive contributions, whilst the occupational therapist started altering her contribution. She had at one time worked exclusively in a hut adjacent to the unit, emerging therefrom only to attend ward conferences and community meetings. Subsequent to membership of the T-group, she saw herself as working on the ward in closer relationship with both staff and patients, in a role more appropriate to the patients' needs. Traditional suspicions and hostilities which exist between nurses and occupational therapists were forgotten and she substituted ordinary clothes for her uniform at the same time as the nurses shed theirs.

The gains for the patients were not so clearly evident. The greater involvement of all members of the team with the patients was an obvious gain. On the other hand, there was, to my way of thinking, far too much ECT being given on the unit, and some other physical treatments such as continuous narcosis, were a good deal in vogue. The reasons for this were complex. The hospital as a whole had a deep and lingering tradition of using physical treatments for the treatment of almost all inpatients. Disturbance in long-stay patients was controlled by ECT and drugs and there was an overall emphasis on control. By the time that I left the unit, it seemed to be divided. One group of patients, with their attendant doctors, were receiving ECT and drugs, the remainder, some of whom included the physical treatment group, were involved in some kind of group or individual therapy. There was a certain amount of persecution of this latter group of patients by certain members of the staff and sometimes by the night nurses, largely on the grounds that they 'weren't having any treatment' or 'it was time they were home and back at work'.

In summary, therefore, it would probably be fair to say that the staff T-group helped the patients to a limited extent, but that the objectives set out under 'Objectives in Psychiatry' were only partly achieved.

For the staff the gains were of a different order. The ward sister became much more confident and developed warmer and closer relationships with her colleagues and with the patients. The meetings were held in her office and at first she remained in her accustomed chair — ready as she said to get out of the door if things got too threatening. One of the social workers, whose approach was shy and diffident at most times but occasionally brash and outspoken on others, started to say how much any communication with the senior staff terrified her. Later she attended the group work course and eventually she greatly improved in confidence and treated the other staff as equals.

It might be an interesting commentary to see what has happened to the original members of this staff T-group. The sister is now working as a community nurse in Southampton, with much satisfaction to herself and she vows she will never return to the parent hospital. The occupational therapist married and alas, departed for London where she is reported to be much less happy in another less therapeutically orientated unit. The social worker referred to above is now working in Nigeria and recently sent us a long and interesting account of her work which I am sure she would not have attempted three years before. The senior registrar was the doctor most deeply committed to physical treatments. He attended the group regularly, got himself involved in frequent altercations with more therapeutically minded staff, and eventually departed, unchanged in his attitudes as far as could be seen. One of the registrars underwent a great deal of personal growth and is now an active member of the adolescent unit which is very committed to a therapeutic approach. One of the senior nurses had a great deal of difficulty on the unit and subsequently left for another unit. It was not until she had afterwards attended the group work course that she was able to appraise her ward T-group experience and to become a really effective member of a therapeutic team. Those who remained on the unit have perhaps been the most conservative members, although they are not necessarily those least open to change.

Staff T-Group at Southampton Day Centre

I propose to conclude this chapter with an account of a staff T-group at the Southampton Day Centre, with which I have been associated for the past nine months. This particular period carries us through what have been to date the greatest and most dramatic changes at the Day Centre and is therefore possibly atypical. The staff group made important and significant contributions to those changes, as will be seen.

The Day Centre in Southampton started about six years ago. Its style and philosophy was modelled on that of the parent hospital 13 miles out of town. It was set up as a ward of the hospital, with a 'day room', 'dormitory' (containing 12 beds and used for the recovery of patients who had ECT), and an 'occupational therapy department'. There were facilities for ECT to be carried out on a fairly large scale, although most of the patients having ECT had been referred from the outpatient clinics which used the same building. The Day Centre staff, however, looked after the ECT patients and 'did ECT'. Not only was the unit run like a ward, but it was in many ways like a chronic ward. The original sister was recruited from a long-stay ward of the parent hospital and after a year or so at the Day Centre returned to another long-stay ward where she still is. There was no doctor in regular charge of the unit, but, as in a chronic ward, one of the consultants visited twice a week. The patients were also largely chronic psychotics. The original staff consisted of nurses, an occupational therapist, and a ward maid. There was no social worker and no proper medical cover, no training facilities for the staff and no community nurses.

Subsequently, a charge nurse was appointed in place of the sister, who attended a group work course and the advanced course. A part-time assistant psychiatrist was appointed to the Day Centre about two years ago and she has attended the group work course. A part-time social worker was appointed who has also, quite recently, attended a T-group course, and a second occupational therapist has been appointed. The latter has not attended a T-group course and does not intend to do so. Of the original staff at the Centre who remain, none has attended a T-group course.

Another development which took place subsequent to the opening of the Day Centre was the appointment of a so-called community nurse. I say so-called because his appointment and the development of his eventual role came about in rather an odd way. About three years ago, more and more patients, mostly schizophrenics, were being discharged from the hospital who were having injections of long-acting phenothiazines at two-, three- or four-weekly intervals. A weakness in this programme lay in ensuring that the patients received regular injections, a requirement, which, interestingly enough, took precedence over regular psychiatric or social work interviews. A state-enrolled nurse was, therefore, appointed to give the injections and to visit patients who failed to attend. Being enthusiastic and community-orientated, he not only cared for a large number of the schizophrenics in the community but he also cared for a considerable number of other psychiatric problems occurring in people referred from several sources. He thus became Southampton's first community psychiatric nurse.

After the part-time assistant psychiatrist had completed her group work course, she started a staff group at the Day Centre. This almost immediately ran into difficulties, due entirely to the impact of the wind of change on the fabric of an old-settled way of psychiatric philosophy with its emphasis on patient control, management, illness and referral-discharge procedures.

In October 1971, I became the first consultant to devote a substantial amount of time to the Day Centre and I had the additional advantage that it was my principal commitment and that I had no clinical responsibilities at the parent hospital. At that time, I found that the situation was that the Centre was being run as an occupational therapy craft-dominated unit. It was virtually being run by the two occupational therapists, in the sense that they had the care of most of the patients for the greater part of the day. The nurses, of whom there were three whole-time and one part-time, together with the doctor, spent most of each morning 'doing' ECT so that they found it very difficult to establish roles and to form relationships with the Day Centre patients. The patients carried out craft work in an 'occupational therapy department' which consisted of part of the area of the Day Centre closed off with sliding doors. These doors were never opened, but there was a wicket door on one side, also kept closed. The nursing and other staff felt that they were intruders in the 'department' and seldom went there. During the afternoons, the patients engaged in 'activities', mostly if not entirely organised by the staff, consisting of play reading, 'musical appreciation', poetry reading and 'health and beauty'. In a similar way to the parent inpatient unit, a dichotomy had evolved between the physical and the therapeutic, as there were several active therapy groups in being, which met three times a week, and to which the staff had a considerable commitment. There were no community meetings, however, and the patients appeared to have little say in how the Centre was run. Staff meetings were held twice a week in a separate room at which prospective new patients were interviewed and slotted into the organization. One found that if they were not allocated to occupational therapy that they tendet to sit around for long periods in the day room without contact with the staff.

Such a set-up allowed the nurses to retain as much as possible of their traditional roles and to opt out of direct contact with the patients. The social worker, too, had allowed herself to take on much other work, unrelated to Day Centre patients.

It was clear that a number of changes were necessary, and over the next few months the following things happened. New nurses were appointed who had responsibility for ECT, thus divorcing this from the Centre, both physically and psychologically. A part-time registrar was appointed, an important move since not only were there now three doctors working at the Centre, but he was in a training post and, therefore, training began to assume greater importance. Before October, student nurses had come so irregularly and briefly to the Centre that it had been impossible for them to become involved in any of its more therapeutic activities. After October, they came for periods of three months, in regular batches of between four and six. A second community nurse was appointed and there are plans for more. Something had to be done about the more chronic patients whose needs were for a social rather than a therapeutic environment. This was met by forming a satellite day centre at a local church hall and this has been a particularly satisfying enterprise since it was a joint endeavour between the local authority, the hospital management committee and the church authorities, three institutions not always noted for co-operating harmoniously together.

An art therapist was appointed to the Day Centre with whom I had previously worked at the parent hospital.

Whilst these physical and administrative changes were being got under way, the staff T-group continued to meet. At first I was welcomed as the one who would solve all their difficulties and, indeed, I had been anxiously invited to attend some of the staff group meetings before I started work at the Centre. It might be useful to say at this point who were the members of the staff group when I joined it. There was a charge nurse and the three staff nurses. One of these left shortly after I came and was replaced by a young staff nurse who brought with her an open-minded community-orientated approach. There were the two occupational therapists, there was the assistant psychiatrist, joined after three months by the registrar. Also in the new year the art therapist joined the group. The community nurse was a member, joined later by the second community nurse. The social worker was also a member, and with myself the group was complete, thirteen members in all, fairly large for a T-group. Attempts had been made to bring the ward maid into the group before I arrived, which had ended in anger and frustration. Attempts were also made to bring at least one of the secretaries in, but these failed and the issue has not been raised lately. A current issue is whether student nurses should join not easy to resolve in view of the size of the group, but they do have their own T-group with the charge nurse and the nursing officer, both of whom have attended the group work course.

For the first few months the staff T-group set the task of getting itself welded into a group and gave this as its reason for not increasing the membership. This goal was partly successful, but was punctuated by bitter and disabling quarrels, usually between different pairs of staff. The group as a whole did little to support attacked members and issues were seldom resolved. The inability of the group to resolve anything probably lay in its inability as a team to alter the general direction of the Day Centre. We had talked from time to time of training days and of having an intensive T-group with an outside trainer, but nothing came of these suggestions at first. Clearly, the group had rendered itself impotent and it continued to look to me as its declared leader, for a way out. At the same time they were saying, in effect: 'Don't hurt anybody, and nobody must leave.'

After about five months of observation, soul searching and thought, I started to have discussions with the staff. I had these separately with the different occupational groups. At these meetings, I tried to find out how they saw their roles at the Centre, whether they were satisfied with them and how they would like to change them. I also put certain proposals for change to them, and asked for their reactions. These proposals arose partly out of the nursing changes, the implications of which were that the nurses now had time to give to their patients, and partly out of my need to change the Centre from a rigidly organised occupational unit into one more therapeutically orientated. It may be worth mentioning at this point that when I use the word 'therapeutic' I mean to convey a process which is primarily concerned with personal interaction, which takes into account unconscious and non-verbal processes, and which is appropriate to the needs of the patient seen in his full context as a whole person. As most of these criteria were not being met, I was proposing changes which would, I hoped, start to meet them. In short, the proposals were that we should divide into two smaller teams, each with a group of patients not more than 25 in number, and that the staff should abandon traditional roles with the patients and become therapists in the sense mentioned above. From the practical points of view, the teams would get together with the patients and plan their own programmes. I also suggested that the whole Centre should be opened up and that all the equipment and facilities should be available to all. I thought that most group activities and individual interviews should take place in the patients' area (with the exception of therapy groups) and that new patients should be welcomed by two or three members of each team and not have to face a large group of staff.

These proposals met with resistances from most people and with shock by some. We were also rapidly approaching the intensive two-day staff group with *Peter Smith,* which itself created anxiety although it allowed some of the issues to be put off. What did happen in the staff group was that the divisions in the staff which had simmered for four years and which had boiled up from time to time could no longer be ignored. The occupational therapists came out strongly and unequivocally on the side of tradition, adherence to the code of their association, and the insistence that the patients were there for 'treatment'. The nurses were bewildered, for, as the charge nurse said: 'I haven't a role now.' The general feeling was that the issue was whether to go along with me or not. Before we knew where we were, the two-day T-group was upon us.

During the first day, the principal issues rested on questions of trust and unity. The day ended hopefully with expressions of mutual confidence and the hope that we could all stay together and work the new 'system'. On the following morning, it seemed appropriate to define some objectives, and these were spelt out by various members of the group. 'Better selection and assessment of patients', 'greater exchange between members of staff', 'more patient power', were some of them. It seemed as if we might be getting somewhere. We then went on to consider some solutions, how these objectives might be achieved. Immediately, in the last session of the two days, a series of objections, anxieties and vetoes were created. The occupational therapists said that in their charter they were consultants to the nurses, there was a violent and deeply mistrustful exchange between four members of the group. The two days ended in deep frustration and anger, shared by our trainer. One of the more gentle voices during that last session came from the nurse, who said: 'Couldn't we open back the doors into occupational therapy, it would make such a difference.'

The next day it seemed as if trust had prevailed after all. The big doors dividing 'occupational therapy' from the 'day room' were opened, never to be closed again. From that time on, traditional occupational therapy never took place. A few patients finished off work which they were doing and some of the many locked cupboards belonging to 'OT' (occupational therapy) were opened. It seemed essential to reorganise the Centre, and we rapidly arranged ourselves into two teams, balancing each team for occupational discipline and sex as far as we could. The patients were divided into two groups attached to the staff teams. From that time on, nearly all meetings and patient interviews took place in the patient area. In the staff group, we retired to lick our wounds and assess what had happened. But all was not well. Whilst the nurses, social workers and doctors worked hard and made several sacrifices to make the project work, the occupational therapists were deeply unhappy and disturbed. They retreated as far down to the end of their department as they could, they remained close together and sat next to one another in meetings whenever possible. When asked what they were doing they said they were stocktaking. Easter came and several of us were on leave. When I came back two weeks later, I found that the senior OT had announced her resignation and the basic grade OT had announced her pregnancy. The result of this was expressions of guilt and anger. The angry feelings came from the staff who felt that the OT should declare what they were prepared to offer, but it appeared that they were prepared to offer nothing. The art therapist was also disturbed, as her way of working had hitherto been in a closed department without intrusion, but she adapted well to the new system and eventually declared that it had advantages. She is currently playing a very constructive role in the staff T-group.

Currently also, the situation is that the senior OT has left and the one who is pregnant will leave in about three months. It is of great psychological interest that an almost exactly parallel situation has been happening within the OT department of the parent hospital, which concurrently has almost disintegrated. It seems that a sad and unhappy chapter in staff/OT relationships is ending, and that, in most instances, group work techniques have contributed nothing to personal growth within that discipline.

One of the preoccupations of the staff T-group has been our relationship with the parent hospital. The staff expressed a great need to develop their own roles and interpersonal relationships without interference. For all, with the possible exception of myself, a constantly expressed fear was that of being 'sent back' to the hospital. The two OT shared this view and declined the option to go to the main hospital. There were feelings that the hospital administration, being committed to inpatient care, had no understanding of a community-orientated service, and saw no advantages in the formation of a small, highly trained, closely knit specialist team. The uncertainty and the knowledge that we could never remain as a settled team, has, in my view, much increased the difficulties of running the Centre and of establishing close working ties. Our experience as tutors on the group work course has proved the value of a small specialist team working together for several years. Present policy dictates that nurses will move every two years, a policy whose implications for the organization as a whole appear to have not been thought through sufficiently. One thing is clear, and that is that the parent hospital sees the need for control of the Day Centre. I did once suggest that it would be more sensible for the nurses at the Centre to be, for administrative purposes, under the Royal South Hants Hospital, which happens to be next door. This met with such a violently hostile reaction that I have not cared to mention it again. It seemed however, a rational suggestion, particularly as the new psychiatric inpatient unit, which will be part of the new University Hospital Croup, will open opposite the Day Centre in three years.

Summary of the Contributions Made by the Staff T-Group to Personal Development

Any assessment of the gains for staff in terms of personal development is bound to be subjective, as we used no objective tests. The principle gains appeared to be increased confidence and a more open attitude to change. Some people, largely on account of personality rather than discipline, seemed unable to change, particularly when they had been under the influence of rigid systems for too long. These people, as we have seen, reacted with disturbance and unhappiness to T-groups and may have to leave. Examples of increased confidence are greater ability to tolerate patient contact and patient manipulation and the ability to express opinions and attitudes. Staff also found it easier to identify with unit norms even when these ran counter to hospital practice. For example, the Day Centre staff have successfully resisted an order from the hospital to wear name badges, on the grounds that in a small unit we should tell people who we are.

One might conclude by saying that my own view, supported by the majority of the Day Centre staff, is that the staff T-group is an essential and integral part of a successful therapeutic unit. There is some evidence that the staff T-group is not viable on its own. It needs to be supported by intensive group work courses on the Southampton model and there needs to be a general commitment to group therapeutic methods in the psychiatric services of the area. If groups are to be a living and real experience with real implications for their members, they must expect conflict, emotional disturbance and personal growth. Staff T-groups are no exception. Their existence, therefore, has implications for the parent organization, which must take cognizance of the existence of dynamic forces at work within its units. Less well understood and studied have been the implication of staff T-groups for the wives, husbands and other people with whom the members have close relationships. Our experience has been that they, too, have to adapt to the increased confidence, changes of attitude and personal growth. They may also suffer from the anger and frustration which may be generated. One must perhaps, leave it to those who read this chapter to draw their own conclusions about the value of staff T-groups, from the mass of largely anecdotal data which I have presented.

References

1 *Beers, C.:* The mind that found itself (London 1908).
2 *Bickford, J.A.R. et al.:* In the mental hospital: Lancet *ii* (1955).
3 *Dawson, J.:* The Ha-Ha (Penguin, London 1961).
4 *Freeman, H.:* Closure of mental hospitals. Brit. J. Psychiat. *120,* suppl. (1972).
5 *Fromm, E.:* The fear of freedom (Routledge, London 1960).
6 *Hales, E.:* Like a lamb (London 1958).
7 *John, A.L.:* The study of the psychiatric nurse (Livingstone, London 1968).
8 *Jones, K. and Sidebotham, R.:* Mental hospitals at work (Routledge, London 1962).
9 *Martin, D.V.:* Institutionalisation. Lancet *ii:* 1188 (1955).
10 *McGhee, A.:* The patient's attitude to nursing care (Livingstone, London 1961).
11 *Raphael, W. and Peers, V.:* Psychiatric hospitals viewed by their patients (King Edward's Fund, London 1972).
12 *Robb, B.:* Sans everything (Nelson, London 1967).
13 *Rognow, A.:* The psychiatrists (New York 1971).
14 *Ryder, J. and Silver, H.:* Modern English society (Methuen, London 1970).
15 *Simpson, J.:* The lost days of my life (London 1958).
16 *Stanton, A.H. and Schwartz, M.S.:* The mental hospital (Tavistock, London 1954).
17 Report of the Committee of Inquiry into Whittingham Hospital (HMSO, London 1972).
18 *Wing, J.K. and Brown, G.W.:* Institutionalism and schizophrenia (Cambridge University Press, London 1970).

Author's address: Dr. *Ronald Sandison,* Green Gables, 6 Holly Hill Lane, Sarisbury Green, *Southampton, SO3 6AD* (England)

Interpers. Develop. *3:* 140–151 (1972)

Group Training in Understanding Society: The Mini-Society[1]

G. Hjelholt

Applied Social Psychology, G. Hjelholt Associates, Denmark

In 1968, I started an experiment which I called the mini-society and which continued into 1969 and 1970. The experiment grew out of my work with sensitivity training, but I suppose for myself it was chiefly an attempt to find a better understanding of the psychological and sociological motivating forces that lie beneath the problems of our present life in society.

In the following, I will try to describe briefly the distinctive features of this laboratory experiment, the mini-societies of each year, and sum up some of the impressions I have culled from these very engaging and chaotic experiments.

Each mini-society lasted 12 days. During this time, the 40–60 participants lived together on a peninsula in a large lake in southern Sweden. Surrounded by the lake and Swedish forests, they were rather isolated and could be active in shaping their two-week stay. An old manor-house with two residential wings and five or six smaller houses nearby, along with an old barn as a meeting place, comprised our territory. The houses were at various distances from the main building with the furthest a full kilometer away in the forest.

The participants were chosen from the information given on their enrolment applications or they were recruited from interested organizations, for example, trade unions. On the application form, there was information about sex, age, employment, income, educational background, motivation for wanting to participate, together with how much the applicant would like to pay for participating. In addition, there was a declaration that 'research' was to be carried out during the laboratory.

An attempt was made to select participants so as to ensure a representative sample of society at large, particularly in terms of socio-economic status, age,

1 The editor and author would like to thank Dr. *Gurth Higgin* of the Tavistock Institute for Human Relations for his advice and assistance in the preparation of this chapter.

and sex. In addition, I worked on the principle that for each group there should be other 'relevant' groups present in the temporary society.

In table I, you can see the membership of the groups for each of the three different years.

Upon arrival at the laboratory, the participants were assigned to homogeneous groups on the basis of their age, sex, and socio-economic status. Initially, the groups were located geographically so that we had an urban area, a middle-class area and some poorer districts. Each group had in a way its own territory, and then there were common areas such as the barn and the main building where amusements, a sauna, billiards, etc., were to be found. For the first 2.5–3.5 days there was an orientation programme. First, the participants were encouraged to get to know their own group. Second, to explore the whole society with all the different groups. And lastly, to participate in community meetings and research meetings to be held in the barn.

There was no programme for the remaining time, as it was announced that after the first few days the participants had to lay their own framework and decide what was to happen. After the first few days, people could also move from one group or house to another. In this way, people had a basis for knowing where they felt that they belonged.

Although there was a staff — composed of my colleagues and co-workers — they were to participate as everyone else in the mini-society, facilitating in any way they felt was meaningful.

This laboratory had many similarities to the usual classical sensitivity training or human-relations laboratories. It was held at (1) an isolated place (a cultural island); (2) it was limited in time; (3) there was a staff; (4) the participants were divided into groups by the staff in advance; (5) it cost money to participate; and (6) it was expected that people could experiment with actions, explore relationships, and to a great extent the individual was dependent on himself for what he got out of the experience.

It differed from usual laboratories because there was (1) a greater variation in the backgrounds of the participating groups, both with regard to age and social status; (2) the participants themselves had decided how much they would pay (varying from 200 to 2,800 Crowns); (3) the groups were homogeneously composed and not as mixed as possible; and (4) the exploration essentially dealt with the relationship of an individual group to other groups. In addition, a great many decisions which are usually decided by the staff were left up to the participants.

1968 Experience

The first mini-society was launched from the 4th to the 15th June, 1968. In the advance notice, the word 'society' was emphasised. It read:

'In the beginning of this two-week laboratory each participant is placed in one of five groups in the society. Here we shall try to create a small society which partially reflects the outer world with its groupings and problems. We will have opportunities to learn about ourselves in our group and our relationships with other groups, since this is our purpose. With others, our group and the whole system, we shall explore the boundaries and distances in our society. Our exploration need not exist solely to collect knowledge about things, but here we have the conditions and a chance to affect the system and to change it.'

There were five groups. The first group was composed of five men and five women students from the same teacher's training college. Then there was a teacher group of four men and three women, who came from the University of Copenhagen, where they had been very active in the recent student demonstrations. From their composition, these two groups could be characterised as closed groups. The next two groups were more loosely put together and more closely resembled neighbourhood groupings in the outer society. The participants did not know each other beforehand, age varied somewhat, and there was a large status differential. One of these groups had in common that they had completed enough schooling to qualify for university admission; there was a touch of internationalism with two Dutch and two Americans participating, and they all held professional jobs (teachers, psychologists, etc.). The second group was a bit older, and there was a strong element of trade unionism in the form of active shop stewards. Economically, they were certainly as well off as the others, but because of their age and education, they had no great ambitions for rising social status.

The fifth group, the staff group, consisted of eight people divided in two age groups: psychologists/psychiatrists who served as helpers, and two younger people, a secretary and a research assistant.

After each group established themselves in their respective houses, everyone gathered for the first community meeting with an introduction, which corresponded to a brief run-down on the purposes of the society (at the same time, they were given a loose schedule for the first three days). On the programme, time was set aside for 'home groups', so they had some undisturbed time for exploration (where they could visit each other) and for community meetings where research and presentation of the results could take place. The first activity of the groups was for each group to choose a name, which it would be known by, and which characterised the group. The professional neighbourhood group called themselves *Babel,* the second neighbourhood group *1968,* the young students *4th June,* and the teacher training college students *Theodorians* after the name of the founder of their college. The staff group chose the name *Wanderers* in order to suggest that they would be moving around.

Since there was a bit of a framework, the first days were orderly and had in fact the character of a somewhat structured sensitivity-training laboratory, where the older *Wanderers* had the role of consultants for the four groups. But when 'moving day' came and the whole society had to make up their minds as to how they should use their time and capital, the drama really began.

The *Wanderers* split up into a *Consultation Centre* and *Lonesome Wanderers*. The *Theodorians* announced that they had changed their name to *No Name* and moved out on a little island from which the others had to fetch them back. The *4th June* who had stayed abreast of the times, had changed their name with each changing day, i.e. *5th June, 6th June,* etc. This group was very active at the community meetings and lived up to its calling as 'revolutionaries'. They sought contact with *1968,* but without getting any particularly warm reception. As in the story, *Babel* disintegrated. There was no chance for growth and development here.

A document from *1968,* which they wanted the others to respond to at a community meeting, reflects the problems people were working with and, at the same time, it indicates the group used as a support in the society:

(1) What characterizes this society?

(2) How can this society be integrated?

(3) What are the groups' attitudes toward the 'mini-society' at various stages in the development?

(4) How can we put together groups according to individuals' desires and needs?

(5) How can we co-operate across the existing groups?

(6) Is it possible for group *1968* to solve a concrete problem together with the group *4th June?*

(7) How do you establish a leadership which assures that development possibilities are not frustrated?

(8) How do we find a problem we would like to solve?

(9) Do the groups here want to have anything to do with each other?

(10) Can we form new home groups?

One theme that cropped up again and again was the question of responsibility for concrete events. At a community meeting, I reported that damage had been done to furniture and fixtures and asked for guidelines for how this should be paid. Some groups expressed surprise, others almost anger, that I had not obtained insurance so they could experiment 'without consequences'. *1968* was the group that handled the practical problems most straightforwardly and also suggested the solution that settled the problem of damages: equal joint liability. But this meant that the poorest ended up paying for what the middle class destroyed.

After this first summer, there was a general impression that the geographical layout of groups was good. The distances between them, which encouraged them to make contact, made it possible for us to bring central problems of the society to the surface. At the same time, I had a feeling that just as individuals act on unconscious levels, our behaviour here reflected unconscious social desires and anxieties. Within the staff group, the development of the society was characterised as a change from an 'incendiary' to a 'building' attitude. After initially encouraging the exploration of differences and confrontation between groups, the staff tried to help them find a common ground for co-operation.

1969 Experience

The main recruiting in 1969 aimed at getting younger people with other than academic tendencies. We were looking for those who were getting a practical education or had dropped out of the educational system. The other groups were collected around this basic group. Characteristically enough, the ten young people took the name of *X*, and they kept this name throughout their entire life in the mini-society. The mixed middle-class group was also younger than the year before (see table I). There was a difference of almost ten years and here we had our first married couple. This group was called *Duodenum*. The academic, internationally arrayed group had the same age distribution as the year before. They called themselves *Will*, which certainly sounded more promising than *Babel*. There was an institution group of six people from Denmark Radio. In the beginning, they called themselves *Krrerr*, after the static sound on radio, but later changed to the *Beagle Band*, characters well known to readers of Donald Duck.[2] Wiser through bitter experience, the professional staff was reduced to five people who, in the beginning, called themselves the *Vikings*, which later became the *Reluctant Vikings*.

The launching of this second mini-society was shorter and less reminiscent of sensitivity training, as the *Vikings* themselves tried to avoid the role of trainers. But this was not so easy, since from time to time they sought refuge in it.

If 1968 had been characterised by problems having to do with (1) the building of a society, (2) the contact between students, teachers, and workers, and (3) the young teachers' insecurity in their profession, 1969 was characterised by 'letting go'. It included 'happenings', a strange marriage and divorce ceremony, an exhibition of the absurd, and many inter-group social events. At the same time, the groups were more flexible. Two persons left *Duodenum*, one of whom sought admission to the *Beagle Boys*. *X* went out into the woods and began to build a hut which they intended to move into, but it remained incomplete at the end of the experience. A work group was formed across the groups

---

2 A group of cartoon Beagle dogs who lived in a prison-like room and who from time to time went marauding into the community, to eventually return to the safety of their secluded room.

Table I. Mini-society participants over three years

1968			1969			1970		
participants	mean age	n	participants	mean age	n	participants	mean age	n
Activist students	23	7	elementary education	19	10	drug addicts	19	8
Teacher students	25	10				American students	19	9
Neighbourhood group, lower middle class	40	11	neighbourhood group	31	12	neighbourhood group	25	7
						neighbourhood group	41	9
Neighbourhood group, academic background	31	10	neighbourhood group	32	9	neighbourhood group	41	10
			institution group	33	6			
Staff group	35	8	staff group	41	5	staff group	43	6
Others, wife and children		4				children's group	8	7
Whole population		50			42			56

to serve the useful function of repairing things that were destroyed, and immediately another group was formed to destroy things so the first would have something to do. In the last part of life in the society, a sort of bureaucratic group was formed. It registered people and published a newspaper. An attempt to put a little order into a chaotic, normless society.

There was great insecurity and dependence on authority throughout the whole experience as a counterpart to the 'letting-go' happenings. The night before the society was supposed to take over full responsibility (after the first loosely structured period), a feeling of impending disaster was prevalent. The groups sat in their respective houses almost all night, without making any contact with the outside. The next morning when the community came together, the fear of the unstructured future had dissipated. The ambivalence of desire for freedom and resentment toward authority for not providing structure resulted in a spontaneous circle dance through the main building and out onto the lawn with loud cries, a choir of voices shouting at me: Ho-Ho-Ho Chi Minh.

The basic theme throughout this experience seemed to be 'generation robbery'. The older members and groups in the society were attempting to relive their adolescence and youth while challenging the younger ones to try and keep pace. For instance, *Will* (the professional group) tried to get *X* (non-academic youth) to dance with them during a session of pop music and to get them to be less inhibited in their bodily movements. This group was also destructive of property in a way they would never have been at home. Even within the staff group, this theme was evident as the *Vikings* split with the two young members who withdrew into their own group contacts and established some links with *X*. The 'generation gap' was most dramatically symbolised in the mixed young and old group, *Duodenum*. They united their two age factions symbolically by a 'happening' marriage ceremony conducted in full view of the community between their oldest and youngest members. It included an elaborate caricature of the role of ecclesiastical authority.

The middle-aged middle class, without the normative restrictions of conventional society, were intoxicated by the chance to get out of a straightjacket, to give expression to their feelings by taking over the standards of the young. The young people were suddenly robbed of their distinctiveness, their youth. They were at a complete loss because now they had nothing for themselves. They said they felt numb and empty. In the middle of the second week, they renewed their stock of pop records — those they brought with them having become common property. And in the middle of the intoxication was insecurity, a general feeling of anxiety: 'Have we gone too far? Who's going to take care of us? At a community meeting, one of the young people called on me to take the power. 'We need someone who will say: everyone goes to bed this evening at ten. We would obey.'

1970 Experience

From the 23rd August to the 4th September, the last experiment on this model took place. As in 1969, the selection placed emphasis on the young. There was a group of children that put their initials together and called themselves *Anpekedochmeka;* a group from the Copenhagen Youth Clinic who were being cured of taking drugs that took the name *Hallucinations.* With the same average age we had a group from America consisting of poor black-white students who were sent by their university but who had worked to pay for the journey. They called themselves *Dilemma.* There were three neighbourhood groups: *The Green Rags and Tatters* and *The Radishes* (both non-professional) and the professional group, who at first called themselves *Association,* later *Establishment.* Under the influence of the children, the staff took the Greek-sounding name *Hyheph.* At the end of a week, a number of break-away individuals (from the *Radishes*) formed a family group called the *Pearl Divers,* while *Anpekedochmeka* was swallowed up by *Rags and Tatters.* One person left *Rags* and joined the *Establishment.*

In earlier years, the participants, after having paid admission according to circumstance, were not required to concern themselves with the society's finance. This was dealt with by the staff group. However, in the previous year, the groups had made comments about wanting 'a real problem' to work with, and at the same time discussions about money, damages, and their attitudes toward these topics brought feelings out into the open which indicated real differences in conceptions about the structure of society. When money had been mentioned, I had an impression that there were stronger feelings of taboo here than about sex. In 1970, one group, the American students, paid the maximum amount (through their institution) and so did most of the members of the *Establishment.* There was a possibility that income and expenses might be able to balance. The manor-house declared itself willing to suffice with 26 full-paying participants.

So, after the first introductory days, I introduced the budget at a community meeting and asked for guidelines as to how the money should be used. Twenty-six could eat at the manor-house. Which? And the others had to keep house for themselves. How much money should they have? After that, it was my task to manage the money and pay out by authorization from the community meeting. The groups' attitudes toward each other and what they considered each group deserved was expressed in concrete figures. Applications for allotments were addressed to the community meeting; among other things, the question of who was or should be privileged was raised. Were the privileged those who ate in the main building at set times, or were they the ones who could decide for themselves when and what they would eat? Pressure was applied to groups. The *Establishment* (professional group), who had their meals prepared and had their beds made, were forced out to the most distant house in the woods where they had to prepare their own food. Later they insisted that this house had to be the main building.

The *Pearl Divers* (family group) and the *Hallucinations* (young, cured drug-takers) made it through the upheavals in the society and developed as distinct groups. The *Pearl Divers* stuck together at the community meetings and gradually assumed a great deal of influence on decisions, while the *Hallucinations* lived their own life-style in their house, where the door was always open. Only toward the end of the mini-society did they attempt to make contact with the community.

The polarization between the two cultures, the *Establishment,* with their 'social' parties and alcohol culture, and the *Hallucinations,* with their hippy, drug culture, and spontaneous and uninhibited behaviour, left their mark on the other groups. The other groups were tugged first in one direction and then in the other. *Dilemma* (poor, black-white American university students), who came from a socio-economic and age group resembling the *Hallucinations,* but by virtue of their presence at university were about to enter the culture of the *Establishment,* felt the tensions so strongly that they found it difficult to move between groups. *The Green Rags and Tatters* (neighbourhood group) were almost torn apart by the fight, which never blossomed out as a confrontation between the two poles. The *Establishment* considered the *Hyheph* (staff group) who, at the beginning declined the usual staff leadership role, as traitors to the established culture. It was only the daily pursuits and the common economic problems that kept the society functioning.

The Different Groups in the Various Mini-Society Experiences

Institutional and Professional Groups

How did the institutional and professional groups fare? Are there any conclusions that can be drawn?

The *Theodorians,* studying to be teachers, were both an institutional and a professional group. This group tried to isolate itself, to retreat, and it was the society that said to them: 'We don't trust you and won't send our children to your schools if you persist in isolating yourself from us.' The institution was powerfully confronted with its mission in the outside world. The older *Beagle Band* (Denmark Radio), who were an institution with a professional background, had defined their role through their choice of name.

Dilemma (poor, black-white American students) was also a closed group on account of its culture and its common university. Here the pressure was strengthened by culture shock, and even if the other groups did not have difficulties with them, they were aware of their cultural isolation. This was reflected in the fact that they never wandered too far away from their house, certainly not far away from 'ear-shot' of their pop music!

The next closed group was the staff group, which had a personal and professional role in common. In 1968, the *Wanderers* split into *Lonely Wanderers* and *Consultation Centre;* that is, the professionals isolated themselves from those who were not professionals and closed in around their profession — which they felt they had to emphasise. In 1969, the *Vikings* became the *Reluctant Vikings*, and the 1970s *Hyheph* hid behind a seemingly Greek word which they never explained.

Neighbourhood Groups

The neighbourhood groups? What were the various forms of association and attraction toward each other?

It was felt that the more or less decent middle class (dentists, teachers, doctors, etc.) brought up in an academic tradition as individual decision-makers could meet and form some kind of common work effort (these were *Babel, Will,* and *Establishment*). With age it became more obvious that they drew together around the things they had in common: their good jobs; their intellectual culture so they could discuss books, films, and wines; and their role as guardians of the 'system'.

The lower middle-class groups, which were not comprised of professionals (*1968, Duodenum* and *Radishes*), did not live so visibly in the society. The stronger the labour representation in the groups, the more it grew into the backbone of the society and raised the practical questions for solution at the community meetings. In addition, they demonstrated a surprising tolerance for the less conventional groups.

One middle-class group, *The Green Rags and Tatters,* however, had a hard time. Whether it was the individual member's loneliness and their desperate attempts to get away from this that did it, I cannot say now. They moved most restlessly about in the society. They drove cars in spite of a distance of only one kilometer, had the children on the roof of the car, and paid frequent visits to other groups in the community. As the community meeting had decided that children should have the same amount of money as the adults, the group hurriedly adopted as many children as possible, but then ignored them.

Investigation of families have played a small part in this society experiment. The first year, we had a family with a baby and a mother with a daughter, but they belonged to the staff group. In the second society, there was a married couple in one of the neighbourhood groups. The wife broke out of the group and applied to another group, while the husband wandered about bewildered, until he later applied for a good solid job in the administration group. In 1970, there were more children and families, both broken and intact. One family formed its own group, the *Pearl Divers,* and tried to collect other children around them. A rebellious daughter joined another group, however.

The children were pretty much left up to themselves, and even though many talked about them, as we do in this 'children's century', all the groups forgot them when it was time to make a decision. The children had to draw the other's attention to their existence from time to time. It has been mentioned that *Rags and Tatters* used the children to gain economic advantages, but otherwise they let the children look after themselves. One group, *Dilemma,* arranged a children's party. The children seemed to thrive in spite of the grown-ups. They could move from one place to another and here they had a much greater chance to be a part of everything that happened; they were not restricted to just one part of existence. Is it the children who get the most out of collectives and compound families, while the pressure is greatest among the adults? On successive investigations of the effects of the mini-society, there is much evidence that family situations are altered in this respect, that the children take a more active part in the upbringing of their parents.

Special interest has been dedicated to youth. How does a young person fare in society, what has an influence on him/her, what becomes of him/her?

The *4th June,* the closed action group with school-leaving certificates, dissatisfied with the state of things, held their own through crises and resistance. They guarded their standards and their norms jealously, while others, both the *Theodorians* of the same age and the older members of *Babel,* tried their hands at being emancipated. It did not go as well, however, for the younger people in *X,* who had no common goal or any education. They tried to influence the society, but were simply knocked down by the overwhelming interest and take-over of their life style by *Will* and the *Beagle Band.* Depressed, they closed themselves in, sought other groups, or went to pieces.

With age *X* might become *Green Rags and Tatters;* or they could pull out of society and live with their own culture, isolated in a semi-fantasy world as did the *Hallucinations;* or the *Establishment* could patronisingly help them to come in and take up establishment standards; or else they could become the slightly rootless, artistic candidates for the middle class.

Conclusions

Reflecting on the outcomes of the experiment in group training for understanding the social roles and forces in society, a number of points come to mind with respect to the role of the staff and my own role. Although the staff group participated on an equal basis with the rest of the participants — they did not get any form of compensation and they involved themselves in the research activities of the society — they found themselves in dual-membership roles. On the one hand, they were to gather information and impressions from the groups in the society and to help and facilitate development and, on the other hand, they were encouraged to participate in those activities that they felt met their own needs as individuals. It is extremely difficult to do both of these things simultanously; one can either become involved and absorbed in an ongoing group or one can cling to observations and impressions and the protection of the trainer role. This was particularly noticeable with the staff and the professional groups; the staff identified with the groups of professionals and yet they tried to dissociate themselves from the professional role.

I had the role of 'boundary keeper' taking care of the relationships between the participants and the cleaning staff, and coping with the issues involving the outside world. The battle to test the limits of the community and the outside was fought symbolically 'on me'. I made the unfortunate mistake of allowing myself this 'middle-man' role when I should have left it to the community to solve. In addition, I had the role of initiator of research and feeding back the results to the community. In this way, I intervened in the life of the society and forced the groups to examine certain issues and behaviour.

It may be that these two roles, boundary keeper and active research intervener are necessary and have to be personified. The lack of clearly defined boundaries seemed to allow freedom within the society, and hence exploration and movement. The research focus, in addition, provided the participants with a means of discovering 'where they are at' inside the community which minimised the fantasies people have about other social groups.

This last discovery has the greatest effect on individuals participating in the mini-societies, together with a heightened disinclination to accept social role patterns as being stable. Social actions are reported by participants and they have to cope with attempts at changing institutions, as well as shift in work roles.

As far as I am concerned, the special problem of the role of youth in our society has led me to clarify my own thinking, as I discovered in the mini-society how complex these problems are. My belief is that the mini-society reflects developments in society that we do not ordinarily see because movements in society are much slower. This is the real value of the mini-society, as a diagnostic instrument for society. In addition, those who take part in it can experience the effect of experimenting with other social roles and the difficulties of crossing social boundaries.

The Danish poet, *Piet Hein,* said: 'Man is that animal who himself draws the lines he himself stumbles over.' The mini-society provides possibilities for moving these lines.

Author's address: Dr. *Gunnar Hjelholt,* Vust, *9690 Fjerritslev* (Denmark)

Interpers. Develop. *3:* 152–158 (1972)

Group Training for the Helping Professions: the Hampshire Experience

C.L. Cooper

Department of Psychology, University of Southampton, Southampton

Background

A number of people representing the helping professions – social workers, psychiatrists, nurses, probation officers – contacted the author and several other colleagues at the University of Southampton in 1968 about the possibility of introducing a course on group dynamics. After a series of meetings with the various interested parties in the community, it became clear that these people were asking for more than just 'a course'; in fact, it seemed to us that their demand stemmed from two unmet needs within the social services of the local community (County of Hampshire). The first was the felt-need for an opportunity of improving their own social skills, for increasing their own self-awareness and sensitivity to themselves and their clients. The second was the need to develop links between the various social and medical agencies within the community, as a means of reducing the obstacles and tensions that inevitably follow the presence of more than one caseworker dealing with one client. Inter-group suspicion, conflict and rivalry were beginning to develop within the region and were judged by many as major obstacles to effective individual and community casework. Within this context, a small number of colleagues and I decided on pursuing the matter further by bringing together the senior administrative staff from each of these helping professions from each of the local and county authorities within the Hampshire area. My colleagues consisted of people representing each of the helping professions; there were two psychiatrists, a nurse, a psychiatric social worker, a lecturer in social casework, a tutor in child care, a probation officer, and myself (a social psychologist). We discussed with the authorities the various requests that had been made, and sought their views as to the training and development needs within the community and how they might be met. It was agreed, as a result of this meeting, that we (the staff of eight) should design a group training experience that would attempt to meet the two felt-needs described earlier, which they agreed were the primary concerns of their staff.

Over the next nine months, the staff met on a number of occasions in an effort to design the training programme. Progress seemed to go very slowly, as the staff found that they were having difficulty working together. There were two reasons for this. First, we did not really know one another very well and there were some unexpressed interpersonal conflicts within the group which needed to be resolved. Second, we found that we were reflecting some of the professional rivalries and jealousies of the social services community at large (since we were a microcosm of this larger professional grouping). Once we were able to see these dynamics operating in our own group, we felt that it would help us (as a planning and training staff) to seek advice from an outside consultant. He suggested that we should have a staff T-group, one designed to focus on the interpersonal and professional obstacles within our *own* group. The consultant was to serve as the T-group trainer to our group. This two-day experience took place a week before our final planning session and about a month prior to the start of the group training programme. The staff development group was quite successful and helped us to make explicit our feelings about one another and where each of us saw the obstacles to our own and the group's development. As a result of this experience, it was much easier for us to work as a team (a week later) in making the final decisions about the design of the training programme.

Group Work Training Programme

It was decided that the two main needs of the helping professions could be met by the use of sensitivity training or T-groups, together with certain intergroup and community exercises, and the unique design innovation of weekly follow-up meetings. There were, therefore, two parts to this group training programme. The first consisted of a one-week residential T-group for 40 participants (as equally drawn as possible from each of the helping professions). There were four groups of roughly ten participants in each group with two staff trainers. The following were the aims and methods as described to the prospective participants:

Aims of Sensitivity Training
This programme aims to provide opportunities to increase four closely allied social skills:
Awareness of one's own behaviour in relation to others.
Clear *understanding* of the behaviour of oneself and of others.
The ability to *relate effectively* to others with whom one is in contact.
The ability to relate effectively in situations involving conflict and co-operation between *different groups*.

Methods of Sensitivity Training

Sensitivity training is a participative method, based primarily on work in small groups of up to a dozen members which are often referred to as T-groups, or training groups. In the T-group, the agenda of the group is the behaviour of each member and of the group as a whole. By examining the ways in which group members react to the behaviour of one another, each participant has an opportunity to increase the skills listed above. Each T-group has considerable latitude in determining for itself what areas of its behaviour it wishes to explore, in the light of the preferences of its members.

The T-group is a specialised training setting which, over a period of days, provides a situation in which it becomes increasingly easy for each member to work on those of his interpersonal skills which he wishes to improve. The group does this by developing a safe, accepting climate in which each member's feelings and reactions count for as much as anyone else's.

Each group contains one or two trained leaders. Their task is to foster the development of the appropriate climate for learning, both through example and suggestion. In addition to meetings of the T-groups, the staff will arrange community and inter-group sessions at appropriate times.

It was hoped that this one-week course would go some way in meeting one of the primary needs of the social service community in Hampshire, i.e. of increasing the self-awareness and sensitivity of the participants and, consequently, laying the foundation for improving the individual's relationships with clients and work associates. As far as the second goal of the training was concerned, reducing inter-professional conflict and rivalry, there were a number of exercises built into the training programme that were designed to highlight and explore the issues of professional identification and inter-group co-operation and conflict. If we examine the training schedule (table I), it can be seen that during the course of each day there was at least one such exercise. For instance, in the exercise labelled 'professional roles', the staff trainers designed this session for the purposes of increasing 'professional role empathy'. In each of four corners of a large plenary room, the labels of social worker, probation officer, psychiatrist and nurse were pinned on the walls. Each participant was asked to choose any one of three of the roles (excluding his own) that (for whatever reason) appealed to him/her. Once they had made up their minds, they were asked to assemble near the appropriate label. Then they were asked to discuss a series of questions in the group as if they, in fact, occupied the role themselves. For example, if a social worker had opted 'to be a psychiatrist' and the question under discussion was 'what motivated you to become a psychiatrist', he was encouraged to answer as if he was examining his own motives 'as a psychiatrist'. A number of questions were put forward by the staff for discussion, such as 'What are the advantages and disadvantages of being a ...?', 'What do you dislike most about the people you have to work with?', 'What do you envy and dislike most in col-

Table I. Training schedule

Session times	Sunday	Monday	Tuesday	Wednesday	Thursday	Friday
09.30 to 11.00		T-group	T-group	T-group	non-verbal communi-cations	transfer of learning exercise
11.30 to 13.00		T-group	free period	fantasies of other groups and roles	T-group	discussion of difficulties of transfer of learning
14.30 to 16.00		free period	inter-group exercise	T-group	free period	final T-group
16.30 to 18.00	introduction	profes-sional roles	T-group discussion of inter-group exercise	free period	T-group	
20.00 to 21.30	T-group	T-group	T-group	T-group	T-group	

leagues you are forced to work with on a particular case?', 'What are nurses, psychiatrists, social workers and probation officers like?', etc. After each group had an opportunity of discussing these questions; they were each asked (in a plenary session) to report on the discussion, on each group's answers to the questions. This allowed an exchange of information, some of which was stereotypic and some genuine empathic insight of the roles of the other professions. In addition, it highlighted some of the dynamics that lead to inter-professional rivalry; envy, fear of the competence and insights of others, status, etc.

Another exercise session was devoted to an inter-group experience frequently called the 'fishbowl'. In this session, one T-group sat around another group and observed them for a period of 30 min without intervening. After this period, the observing group provided the observed group with 15 min of feedback on their behaviour, answering some of the following questions: 'To what extent do the members trust each other?', 'How are decisions made in the group?', 'Who dominates the group?', 'Are the members playing games with each other?', etc. The observed group was instructed to listen. At the conclusion of the 15-min feedback period, the observers and the observed were asked to change places and to repeat the 30-min discussion and 15-min feedback sessions. Each group then returned to their T-group for a lengthy discussion of the exercise. Several things are gained from such an exercise. First, the participants find out more about the dynamics of their particular group as seen by another less involved group. Second, they learn more about themselves when they discover that some of the feedback they had given applied more to their group than to the other one. Third, they saw that although both groups were quite different, the dynamics of the groups and the developmental patterns were fairly similar. And lastly, an inevitable consequence of this kind of exercise is that a certain level of inter-group competition develops. Whereas the participants are asked to provide con-structive feedback to the other group (feedback that might help them to grow), they discover that they have tended to be destructive. It was seen that this destructive attitude grew out of intense group identification and it was very easy to observe the connection between the similarities of this group training situation (and its consequences) and their own professional identifications and rivalries.

Another major feature of this training design, which it was felt would add to the two primary aims of the social service workers was follow-up training. After the participants had completed the one-week course, they attended weekly meetings of approximately 1.5–2 h in length for the following 20 to 30 weeks. These meetings served a number of purposes. First, to reinforce the personal learnings that resulted from the T-group course. Second, to provide these people with opportunities of discussing current group work projects of their own. Third, to continue the link between professions within the community. These meetings tended to be, on some occasions, T-group oriented, where participants concentrated on developing their own interpersonal behaviour within the group. On other occasions, it provided a forum for a 'content' (as distinct from a 'process') discussion of individual group work experiences and community ser-vice relationships.

As time went on, however, the group work applications and community interrelationships became the focal point for further T-group activity. It was evident that individuals in the group were bringing up albeit unconsciously, outside group work events and professional rivalries that reflected particular interpersonal difficulties currently active within the training group. In this way, one could see the close and intimate relationship between the world outside and the world within the T-group. The value of the weekly meetings grew as this relationship became more evident.

Group Training Development

The response within the community to this first course and the follow-up programme was very good and we were encouraged by local social service agen-cies, hospitals, etc., to continue to organise and develop this programme on a permanent basis. In addition, other related organisations indicated that they

would like to participate in future activities by sending their staff on this training, such organisations as local education authorities, prisons, the church, and
the youth work service.

This group training experience is now an established annual event in Hampshire but the exercises supporting the basic T-group experience have been altered
to meet the changing needs of the constituents. In addition, the staff have
continually brought in ex-participants as co-trainers, to (1) help them develop
skills in designing and running similar group training courses, and (2) to maintain
the staff's contact with the local social service community and with it's changing
institutions and needs.

A further development took place after the 1971 programme when the
training staff, on the advice of ex-participants and training officers in the relevant agencies, introduced an advance group work course consisting of a series of
ten weekly meetings (of two hours duration). This was intended to supplement
the experiential learning of the T-group by a cognitive input. This course was
restricted to approximately 16 participants, who were divided into two groups
for seminar purposes. All members of this course were expected to have completed a T-group course, either in Hampshire or elsewhere. In addition, they
were required to be currently leading or significantly involved in a group as part
of their professional work. Each meeting was divided into two parts. The first
part consisted of a lecture on an aspect of group work. The second part took
place in seminar groups and took the form of a supervision/consultation session
in which participants were expected to come prepared to present their current
group work experiences as a focus for learning. The following lecture programme
was arranged for the course, the lectures were given by prominent group work
people in the Hampshire area:

(1) The fields of group work. (2) Setting up a group — some theoretical and
practical considerations. (3) The development of the individual and the group.
(4) Leadership. (5) The group as an instrument for learning. (6) Group experiences with patients. (7) Parents' groups. (8) Family group therapy. (9) Organisational development in a hospital setting. (10) Prison and probation groups.

The purposes of this advanced group work programme was twofold: (1) to
meet the furthering cognitive needs of experientially-trained social service
workers; (2) to continue to develop the links between the professions and, therefore, to maintain open and genuine channels of communication within the region.

Future Plans

By 1975, it is expected that a vast proportion of the workers in the helping
professions in Hampshire will have been through the group training programmes
discussed in this article. That is to say, a large number of people will have gained

some sensitivity and insight into their own and group behaviour and will have made some genuine contacts on a long-term basis with other related workers in the community. These contacts will have widened with the introduction of the group lecture and seminar course. But these innovations are only the peak of the pyramid, and what is intended in the near future is a more comprehensive and specifically structured community development programme. This programme, although only in its infancy, would attempt to bring together people who are frequently involved in the same cases as well as establishing permanent 'link-groups' between the various community social services in the region. These latter groups would consist of representatives from each of the services who would meet to discuss issues of mutal concern (particularly inter-professional obstacles). These groups might meet for several months, after which time the membership of the committee would be rotated to allow maximum access by all to other community service workers. In addition, another possible adaptation of the current training design might be the inclusion of the clients/patients into the joint consultation groups and perhaps into the 'link-groups' as representatives of the consumer.

Author's address: Dr. *Cary L. Cooper*, Department of Psychology, University of Southampton, *Southampton SO9 5NH* (England)

Interpers. Develop. *3:* 159–166 (1972)

Varying One's Group Training Style to Take Account of the Setting

P.B. Smith

School of Social Sciences, University of Sussex, Brighton

The behaviour of the trainer in sensitivity training is one of the most systematically under-examined topics in the whole field. Over the years, this author's views have fluctuated wildly, from believing that the detailed content of
what the trainer does in the group does not materially affect the long-term
consequences to believing that trainer behaviour is crucial to the outcome of the
group. This paper will not be an attempt to explore the rather sparse research
literature relevant to this point but to describe the author's somewhat halting
attempts to become more self-conscious about *choosing* a style of training to fit
a particular setting. Such choice was not an urgent priority so long as the bulk of
training was conducted with heterogeneous groups of initial strangers: such settings are relatively well understood and the trainer behaviour required within
them is agreed between a wide range of trainers. The central requirements of
such groups are probably trainers who focus attention on the group, encourage
expression of feelings and reactions, and give the group sufficient autonomy
from the outside world and from the trainer himself.

Sensitivity training is now applied in an enormous range of settings in which
the above prescription would be quite inappropriate. This diversification creates
a situation where it becomes less useful to think of sensitivity training as a
technique which under specified conditions will reliably produce a particular
end-result and more useful to think of it as a craft skill, which needs continuous
adaptation to varying circumstances. The essence of craftmanship is that one has
a clear understanding of the principles underlying one's success in a particular
task, and hence can adapt one's behaviour in response to external demands.

A number of components of the culture of sensitivity training make it
difficult to see it as a craft skill. One problem is the existence of a number of
relatively autonomous schools of thought within the field, each of whom has
considerable investment in believing that their style of training is far more effec-

tive than is that of other schools of thought. Although there is certainly a good deal in common between the approaches of all those involved in sensitivity training, much more energy goes into emphasising the differences rather than seeking to delineate the common craft elements. The dynamics of this process are all too readily apparent in planning meetings of any large sensitivity training programme. A second difficulty is the preference of many trainers for planning their behaviour in a highly intuitive manner. One includes a particular exercise in a training design because it 'feels right'. If another trainer with different preconceptions finds that something else 'feels right' to him, then planning becomes a process of bargaining and interpersonal accommodation. The lack of an explicit craft-based rationale for the training makes it impossible to decide the issue on the basis of training needs rather than of preserving amity between the trainers. The belief that only when trainers' own needs are met will those of their trainees be met frequently appears implicit in planning procedures. However, it is the kind of belief which power figures have maintained in relation to their subordinates for centuries, and is no more likely to be true in sensitivity training than elsewhere.

There are a number of explicit training models available for trainers seeking to be systematic in designing their activities. Consider for instance the Rogerian model. Although it refers to psychotherapy, the three therapist prerequisites of congruence, empathy and unconditional positive regard can be readily treated as prerequisites for a trainer also. Personally, I have never found this particular model too helpful, as I have never been able to see how one can both be congruent and show unconditional positive regard towards someone I dislike. To be sure, it is possible if one happens to be very close to someone, but in situations where one has some ambivalence or hostility there is a definite choice as to whether or not to express those feelings. If one does one is being genuine but hardly showing unconditional positive regard; if not, one is not being genuine, however much unconditional positive regard one expresses.

As it happens, this particular dilemma, whether or not to express hostile feelings in a group at a particular time, is one on which I have frequently felt the need for some explicit guiding model. In a stranger group, I would normally feel that to express myself genuinely was the higher priority. But when working with an intact organisational group, I would be much less likely to express hostile feelings towards the boss of the group, if none of the other members dared to do so.

One model which I have found to be of considerable value in this respect is the *Harrison and Lubin* (1965) confrontation-support model. This maintains that learning occurs in a group where both support and confrontation are present. In other words, if a member finds that someone both likes him and expresses warmth toward him *and* dislikes some aspect of him, this experience generates change. *Harrison and Lubin* (1965) write about the presence of support and confrontation in the group, but I prefer to look at it in more individual terms. If an individual experiences support from one member of his group and confrontation from another, this will not lead to learning. It will more likely lead him to like the person who supports him and dismiss the person who confronts him. Only where both support and confrontation come from the same source will he need to face up to the confronting material.

I regard the support half of the *Harrison and Lubin* (1965) model as the easy part. Given time, autonomy, and the encouragement of the trainer, a group can be relied upon to create a warm, supportive climate. Some groups find it more difficult than others, but these, I shall argue, are those in which some kind of confrontation is structurally inherent. At least within stranger groups, support is easy. Confrontation, on the other hand, varies considerably. Confrontation in the group may derive from the trainer or from the group. In table I, four possible group settings are differentiated, with examples in each cell which I shall be discussing. It should be noted that table I makes no reference to the presence or absence of support in the group. This is a consequence of my view that support as a component of the T-group culture is the easy part to obtain. As a trainer I would not feel it right to take on a commitment to train a group to whom I was unable to offer support. I have occasionally found myself with groups whose own capacity for support was rather low, but I shall not be considering such settings here.

Table I. Varying settings in which I engage in sensitivity training

Group is	Trainer is	
	confronting	not confronting
confronting	groups of undergraduates whom I also teach	intact organisational work groups groups of work colleagues
not confronting	student personal growth workshops	heterogeneous stranger groups

In assigning types of groups to cells in table I, account is taken not so much of the *personal* predispositions of groups or trainers, but rather of pre-existing and continuing role relationships with one another. At the interpersonal level, I assume that most people have the capacity to confront one another if they so wish. The entries in the cells obviously reflect my own situation as a university lecturer: Had I been in some other occupation, the examples in the left-hand column would not be drawn from university settings. I shall now discuss some examples from each of the four cells drawn from recent training experiences. In each setting, my goal is firstly to think through the nature of the setting and then to clarify how I, as trainer, should behave if I am to optimise the possibility of group members' experiencing support and confrontation from the same source.

Both Trainer and Group Are Confronting

For a number of years past, I have organised a three-day residential sensitivity training laboratory for undergraduate students majoring in social psychology. The University of Sussex has 20 such students per year. The programme is scheduled towards the end of the students' second year at the university, at a stage when they also spend time doing course work concerning studies in experimental social psychology. I am a confronting figure to the students because among others I am involved in assessing their final degree results a year later, and more generally because I am in touch with other faculty members at the university. The group situation is inherently confronting to them insofar as it resembles group teaching situations which predominate at Sussex, such as tutorials, seminars, and practicals. In each of these, there is some element of peer evaluation implicit in the setting.

The confronting preconditions for these groups mean that I see my main task in them as that of creating support. This involves both my giving support and also encouraging the emergence of support systems within the groups. It is difficult for me to establish the authenticity of my support. For instance, the groups have always been clearly labelled as voluntary rather than as a course requirement. Voluntariness should signal both that the groups are not related to the assessment system and that, unlike other parts of the degree programme, the groups are based on individuals taking responsibility for their own behaviour. The voluntariness of the groups is, however, sometimes interpreted in other ways by students, who may state that they do not feel really free not to come. In practice, about two-thirds of the students have come in recent years. The groups tend to be very centered on the trainer. His trustworthiness as a person is a matter for extended examination, and the groups often seem unable to explore other issues until some resolution of this issue is achieved. My response to this in terms of programme design is to maximise the amount of time spent in T-groups and not to propose other types of sessions. A sparing use is made of non-verbal exercises within the T-group when they fit in with issues salient in the group. The exercises used are often those which highlight issues of trust or support, such as 'trust falls', 'cradling', 'eye gazing' and the like.

The groups do not feel as exhilarating or 'freeing' as some other kinds, but their effects are often marked in terms of their beneficial effect on later tutorials and seminars. A second effect is often some kind of reorientation of the gulf which many students find between their own experience and the research literature on experimental social psychology.

The Trainer Is Confronting but the Group Is Not

A number of faculty at Sussex recently initiated a programme of personal growth workshops. In their first term, these workshops were attended by more than 100 of the 3,000 undergraduates at the university. The format of the workshops varied, some being residential, others being marathons or week-end groups, while yet others met on a once-weekly basis. The groups were open to all undergraduates in the university, while most of the trainers were teaching staff. The confronting nature of the group leaders does not arise in these groups from specific assessment relationships; it arises rather from the experiences of these students with faculty in general. Student-faculty relations at Sussex are informal compared to those at some other universities. Nonetheless, there exists a considerable distance, which no doubt arises out of the different life-styles of students and faculty. Initially, students in the groups were typically strangers to one another, felt somewhat isolated, and shared a wish to achieve some kind of personal growth or new experience from the group.

The principal difficulty found in these groups was that of developing a sense of shared responsibility for what occurred. Members' orientation tended to carry over from campus culture as a whole, and could perhaps be expressed as, 'It's the leader's job to make this a worthwhile experience for me; if he's not up to it, I'll drop out and try something else.' The problem was one of building a supportive climate in which this 'consumer' orientation was superseded. This was much more effectively achieved in the intensive groups than in the weekly groups. Somehow the leader needs to steer a course between excessive confrontation, which will eliminate from his group those who are not strongly committed to it, and the kind of support which will build very high cohesion but very little carryover from the group into other settings. I personally feel much more at ease in settings where I am not, myself, a main source of confrontation, and will now turn to some of these.

The Trainer Is Not Confronting but the Group Is

This situation arises when one works with intact-work-groups in an organisation other than one's own. This discussion draws on recent experiences with a mental health clinic and with a drug addiction unit run on therapeutic community lines. In the mental health clinic, a number of professional groups — doctors, nurses, social workers and occupational therapists — worked together. They encountered frequent difficulties in building a climate of shared trust. Each professional group felt strong loyalties not only to the clinic but also to their professional training. When one group threatened another, it was easy to fall back on one's professional reference group for protection. In the drug centre, confrontation derived more from the inherent difficulty of the unit's task, the constant suggestions of failure and the all-too-rare indications of success.

In these groups, the trainer's required role is relatively clear to me. The groups are burdened with difficulties and confrontations they dare not face up to. The trainer's task is to generate enough support in the group to make it possible to confront these problems. In order to do this, he does not need a central position in the group, indeed, he is inevitably no more than a transient visitor to it. What he does need is an ability to devise supportive procedures for the group. These may be task-centred procedures or they may have a stronger emotional focus, depending on the culture of the group one is working with. For example, with the mental health clinic group a sequence of activities was used in which they sought to diagnose what problems they were faced with, what possible solutions might be entertained, and what procedures they might use to decide between them. In the drug unit, on the other hand, a sequence of nonverbal exercises focussing on 'helping' and 'empathy' were used. Both interventions were supportive but they were at a level congruent with the group's existing procedures.

In existing groups, one of the trainer's main difficulties is that key events occur before he arrives and after he leaves. These events colour the quality of the intervention, and yet the trainer has very little control over them; indeed, he may not even be told that they have occurred. In the mental health clinic, the director made a proposal for a radical reorganisation of the clinic, just a few weeks before the group met. In the drug unit, the most important issues were 'who should or should not be present at the group', since this effectively determined which issues would be worked on during the group. Thus, the trainer can make an effective contribution to an existing group only if that group establishes an open communication link with him ahead of time. The establishment of such a link is a first test of the trainer's ability to contribute to the client group the support they are seeking.

Another existing organisational group with which I have worked is the postgraduate degree programme in social work at Sussex University. This is a highly cohesive two-year programme admitting around 18 students per year. Although this programme is within my own institution, I do not see my role in it as a confronting one. Assessment plays a minor role in the programme and the students on the programme identify as strongly with their future profession as they do with the University. They have an opportunity to attend a three-day residential sensitivity training programme in their first year. In the second year, I run a course for them entitled 'social group work'. This is designed as an intervention in the social system of the course. The basic procedure involves the use of a one-way observation mirror. The course meets for a half-day per week for about ten weeks. The course splits into two groups. For half the time, group A observes group B, while group B works on their own concerns. These concerns may be interpersonal ones or they may be problems concerning the practice of social group work. After half-time, the groups reverse roles. Each group is charged with making constructive interventions in the other.

The most likely event is that A and B become two groups in 'win-lose' conflict, with each supporting themselves and confronting the others. Since the course group has considerable salience for its members, such a breakdown in it could become quite painful. The situation, therefore, requires that each group develop skills in *confronting* the other group *supportively*. Early on they often comment on how much easier it is to analyse the failings of the other group, while feeling paralysed in developing one's own group. From this point, the groups work towards support and confrontation in combination rather than in opposition.

Neither the Group Nor the Trainer Is Confronting

I have left until last that situation which represents the 'classic' T-group, the heterogeneous stranger group. If confrontation occurs in such groups, it occurs because of the behaviour of the members, not because it is structured into the group. Compared to the other types of group discussed, the attraction of a stranger group is its sheer freedom to develop in a self-determining way. The culture of such a group is to emphasise the common elements in human experience and to cherish the sharing of those elements. The danger of such a group climate is that it fosters a denial that there are any divisive or confronting issues in society. My view of the trainer's task in a stranger group is consequently that his task is to confront the members. He will want to do this in a supportive setting and in such a manner as preserves the individual's freedom to be confronted or *not* confronted, but within this framework he will generate opportunities for members to grow through confrontation. This frequently involves both verbal feedback and non-verbal activities. The non-verbal activities will include a broader range of both supportive and confronting activities.

I have now reviewed instances of groups falling within each of the four cells of my table. Through the use of the support-confrontation model, I have tried to explain how I have started to think about planning my interventions. Thinking about intervention and design suggests a degree of self-consciousness which seems to conflict to some extent with other values of the sensitivity training movement, which I also esteem, such as spontaneity and genuineness. It is my belief that disciplining one's trainer activities within broad frameworks such as support or confrontation, need in no way detract from spontaneity or genuineness. At no point does the model propose that as a trainer one should behave in any way other than how one feels; it does, however, suggest that one should select from among one's feelings some rather than others. The manner in which one chooses to express them is always a matter for spontaneity.

Choosing between one's feelings does imply that one has a range of available feelings in a particular situation to choose between. Consequently, one might argue that the implicit values of this model are that the human condition is one of ambivalence. I find that this fits my own position, but others may feel more at ease with Rogerian unconditional positive regard or Sartrean despair.

Reference

Harrison, R. and Lubin, B.: Personal style, group composition and learning. J. appl. behav. Sci. *1:* 286–301 (1965).

Author's address: Dr. *Peter B. Smith,* School of Social Sciences, University of Sussex, *Brighton, Sussex* (England)

Subject Index

Action planning 101, 102, 105, 111
Action skill 11
Adaptability 82, 83
Affection, need of 11
Aggression 10, 11
Ambiguity 81
    of higher education institution 49
Anger 135, 143
Anxiety 51, 52, 81, 82, 84, 86, 90, 136, 143,
    146
Argyle, M. 15
Argyris, C. 81
Assumption 85, 88, 90
Astrachan, B. 11
Attitudes 83, 101, 105
    patients in psychiatric hospitals
        117–120
    staff in psychiatric hospitals 118–120,
        124, 126, 133
Authority 90, 91, 110, 146
    relations 10, 11
    women and 88
Awareness 82, 83, 105
    development of 45

Bales, R.F. 59
Becket, S. 49
Beckhard, R. 80
Beers, C. 117
Behaviour, examination of own 81
    flexibility of 14, 15
Behaviour change 33, 38
Behavioural skills 17
Bellis, E. 100

Benne, K.D. 80, 85
Bennett, E.B. 61
Bennis, W.G. 16, 80
Berger, M. 70
Bickford, J.A.R. 115
Bion, W.R. 59, 85, 90
Bradford, L.P. 85
Brown, G.W. 115
Brunstetter, P.H. 14–16
Buchanan, P.C. 14–16
Bunker, D.R. 15, 22, 24

Campbell, J.P. 16
Catering industry, choice of research sites 17
    previous research in 14
    social skill training in 13–39, 73
Chammah, A. 62
Chemical industry, T-groups in 73, 80–99
Chin, R. 80
Civil Service, T-groups in 68–79
Clare, J.N. 14
'Cogwheel' system, hospital administration
    115, 116
Communes, children in 150
Communication 10, 68, 101, 105, 164
    networks, 157
        psychiatric hospitals 116, 117,
            119, 120, 127, 130
    of feelings 9, 10, 47, 52, 160
Community development, T-groups and 158
Community groups 55, 91
Community meetings 130, 134, 142
Community needs, related to training goals
    17

Authors' Index